Two-Hour Vests

Mary Jo Hiney

Sterling Publishing Co., Inc. New York
A Sterling / Chapelle Book

Chapelle:
- Jo Packham, Owner
- Cathy Sexton, Editor
- Pauline Locke, Illustrator
- Staff: Marie Barber, Ann Bear, Areta Bingham, Kass Burchett, Rebecca Christensen, Holly Fuller, Marilyn Goff, Shirley Heslop, Holly Hollingsworth, Shawn Hsu, Susan Jorgensen, Leslie Liechty, Ginger Mikkelsen, Barbara Milburn, Linda Orton, Karmen Quinney, Rhonda Rainey, Leslie Ridenour, and Cindy Stoeckl

Photography:
- Kevin Dilley, Photographer for Hazen Photography
- Leslie Liechty, Photo Stylist for Chapelle

If you have any questions or comments or would like information on specialty products featured in this book, please contact Chapelle, Ltd., Inc., P.O. Box 9252, Ogden, UT 84409 • (801) 621-2777 • (801) 621-2788 Fax

Library of Congress Cataloging-in-Publication Data

    Hiney, Mary Jo.
        Two-hour vests / Mary Jo Hiney.
            p.   cm.
        "A Sterling/Chapelle book."
        Includes index.
        ISBN 0-8069-9902-0
        1. Vests.   I. Title.
    TT615.H55   1998   98-14777
    646.4'5--dc21   CIP

10 9 8 7 6 5 4 3 2 1

Published by Sterling Publishing Company, Inc.
387 Park Avenue South, New York, NY 10016
© 1998 by Chapelle Ltd.
Distributed in Canada by Sterling Publishing
c/o Canadian Manda Group, One Atlantic Avenue, Suite 105
Toronto, Ontario, Canada M6K 3E7
Distributed in Great Britain and Europe by Cassell PLC
Wellington House, 125 Strand, London WC2R 0BB, England
Distributed in Australia by Capricorn Link (Australia) Pty Ltd.
P.O. Box 6651, Baulkham Hills, Business Centre, NSW 2153, Australia
Printed and Bound in the United States
All Rights Reserved

Sterling ISBN 0-8069-9902-0

contents

learning
the
basics

learning the basics

tools needed

- buttonhole scissors or utility knife
- embroidery scissors
- fabric marking pen
- fabric scissors
- hand sewing needles
- iron & ironing board
- loop turner
- masking tape
- measuring tape
- paper scissors
- pin cushion
- pointer & creaser
- press cloth
- rotary cutter & board
- seam ripper
- sewing machine & accessories
- straight-edge ruler
- straight pins
- thimble, optional
- thread

1. planning makes perfect

In order that the sewer be successful in making any of these vests in two hours, it is recommended that small goals be set before beginning.

1. All of the pattern enlarging should be done at one time.

2. All of the cutting from the fabrics should be done at one time.

3. When stitching, all similar steps should be done simultaneously.

These three easy steps will help in the planning stages and, when working in an assembly-line fashion, each basic vest offered should be able to be made in the two-hour time frame.

Remember that pressing is key — never skip a pressing step. This is the single most important aspect for achieving a professional result.

Keep in mind that it is easy to fully line a vest and a terrific way to achieve professional results.

The overall goal should be to do the best possible work in the shortest period of time and to do this, all unnecessary steps must be eliminated!

2. learning the terms

Grain:
The lengthwise and crosswise direction of threads which compose the fabric.

Lengthwise Grain:
The vertical, more sturdy threads which the crosswise threads are worked over and under.

Crosswise Grain:
The direction of threads that run from selvage to selvage, at right angles to the lengthwise grain threads. Crosswise grain generally has a slight amount of give.

Selvage:
The narrow, flat, woven border resulting at both lengthwise sides.

Straight of Grain:
The direction of the lengthwise threads running parallel to the selvage. Place all grainline arrows along the lengthwise grain.

Bias:

The diagonal intersection of the lengthwise and crosswise threads. Fabric cut on the bias grain possesses a great amount of elasticity, similar to the stretch of a knit. True bias exists at the 45° angle when lengthwise and crosswise grains are perpendicular.

3. straightening fabric ends and grain

Before beginning to cut any garment from fabric, straighten all fabric ends and fabric grain.

Gently pull a crosswise thread so fabric begins to pucker along the thread line. Cut along puckered thread across the fabric width.

Fold fabric in half, matching selvage edges, after fabric ends have been straightened. If ends are not even, open fabric out and gently pull fabric at opposite corners to the direction the fabric ends slant. Fold in half again and check ends. Lightly steam.

4. enlarging patterns

Every pattern provided will have an enlargement percentage given.

Enlarge patterns, according to that percentage, at any copy center onto blueprint size paper.

Using paper scissors, cut the pattern out. Make certain the correct size of pattern (small, medium, or large) is used.

5. cutting patterns from fabric

Fold fabric in half, right sides together, matching selvage edges. Position patterns onto fabric aligning lengthwise grain pattern markings and utilizing the fabric with as little waste as possible. Make certain all necessary pattern pieces and bias cuts have been accounted for.

Beginning with pattern grainlines, pin pattern to fabric, measuring from pattern grainline to selvage edge to make certain piece is straight and equally distanced on the grain. Pin remainder of pattern to fabric by smoothing pattern along fabric from center to outer edges. Cut pattern from fabric — automatically cutting a left side and a right side of each pattern piece.

Cut seam align-

Pin pattern pieces to fabric so fabric is used economically. Make certain that grainlines are parallel to selvage edges and work from the center to the outer edges.

ment notches $1/4"$ into seams. This method is a very quick way to mark notches.

Make certain to cut bias strips for binding edges along the true bias. To find the true bias, fold a fabric corner down so the selvage edge (lengthwise grain) meets cut fabric edge at crosswise grain, forming a 45° angle on the fabric piece. Pin to secure. Cut along edge of fold with fabric scissors. Fold bias cut over on itself. Use a rotary cutter and straight-edge ruler to cut a clean edge along bias. Measure the length of one bias edge. Divide this length into the total length needed as specified in the individual vest instructions. This will determine the number of bias cuts to make. Measure and mark bias into specified widths/

cuts necessary. Use rotary cutter to cut marked bias strips.

6. marking fabric for darts and pockets

The quickest way to mark fabric for darts, pockets, and

other important placements is with a fabric marking pen. Place a straight pin through the pattern and the fabric at each construction marking. Lift the pattern away from the fabric, except at the construction markings. Place a dot at each pin on the

Use a fabric pen to mark darts, pocket placements, and other important construction markings onto wrong side of vest pieces.

wrong side of the fabric. Turn the piece over and mark the opposite vest piece in the same manner. Make certain to mark both fabric layers. Remove the pins as you work, after marking the second side.

A fabric marking pen may not show up on some fabrics. The best alternative would be to use "tailor tacks." Do this by placing a straight pin through the pattern and the fabric at each construction marking.

Using double, but not knotted thread, take a small, loose running stitch through both fabric layers at mark. Take a second loose running stitch at mark so that stitch forms a loop. Continue at all marks.

Separate fabric layers to reveal the tailor tack. Pull apart slightly, then cut tailor tack apart.

7. using interfacing

Interfacing is necessary for nearly all vests to help maintain a properly shaped garment.

There are many types of interfacing available, but for the fastest method with the best results, choose a lightweight woven fusible interfacing.

Trim the interfacing seam allowances as designated for each vest to eliminate the bulk that fusible interfacing can create.

The bias strips cut from fusible interfacing will not be one continuous length. When fusing in place, begin a second piece where the first piece has ended. Trim the second piece so it will be flush to the end of the first piece. Do not overlap fusible interfacing bias strips. It is not necessary to trim the seam allowance from fusible bias strips.

8. sewing seams

Unless otherwise specified, all seams have a 1/2" seam allowance.

Pin the seams, right sides together, placing pins at right angles to seamline, with pin heads facing outward. It is possible to stitch over pins, but remove them when necessary.

Backstitch when beginning and ending a seam. To save time, always trim threads immediately after having stitched 3" into the seam.

Usually, several seams from various

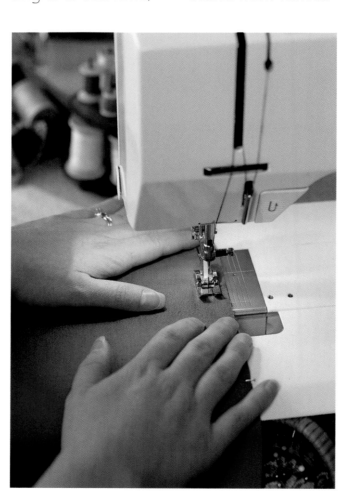

Pin and stitch seams, right sides together. Place pins at right angles to seam with pin heads facing outward.

vest parts can be stitched simultaneously. When stitching several seams, chain the seams together, then clip apart when finished. Remember to backstitch at the beginning and ending of each seam.

Corner and pointed seams need to be reinforced with a second row of stitching placed directly outside of the first stitched row and 1" in either direction from the corner or point. Fabric can then be clipped right to the inward or outward corner.

Additionally, take one or two stitches, depending on the weight of the fabric, across a corner point, rather than stitching right up to the corner.

Trim bulk from seam allowances that involve enclosed seams, such as collars. Cut diagonal corners across the pointed end as well as trimming on either side of the point.

Grade seam allowances where multiple fabric edges are involved, such as neck edges with collars. This is done by trimming each fabric layer slightly larger than the previous one.

Clip all inward curves at $1/2$" to 1" intervals and notch bulk from outward curves. Do not clip past the seamline.

To press a seam, begin by pressing over stitches at the seam to blend the fabric layers, then press seams open, or as specified in the individual vest instructions.

When working with an edge-pressed seam, press it open prior to turning piece right side out. For instance, an edge seam is located at the front closure edges, vest bottom edges, or pockets.

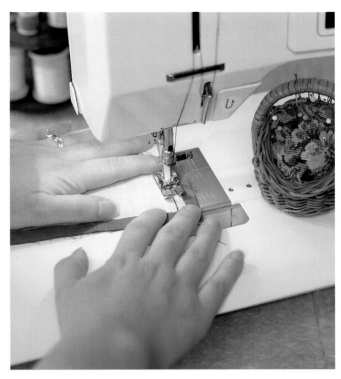

Reinforce corner or pointed seams with a second row of stitching placed 1" in either direction of the corner and directly to the right of the first row of stitches.

Trim away bulk from corners with a diagonal cut.

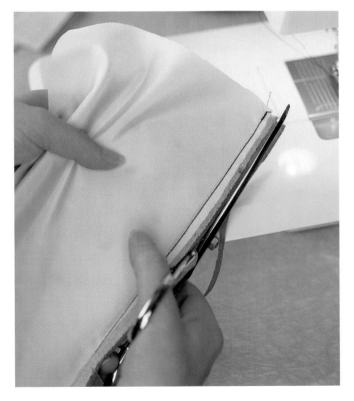

Grade seam allowances by trimming fabric layers slightly larger than the previous layer.

First, press the stitched line flat to blend. Then, fold open the top seam allowance layer and press. This does not press a seam open in the traditional manner, but it exposes the seam and enables it to be pressed flat more easily when turned right side out.

Understitching is done onto the right side of the lining or facing. Machine-stitch as close to the seamline as possible through all seam allowances. Turn the lining or facing in and press seamed edge.

For the neck, armhole edges, and vest points, a row of stitching placed $1/8$" in from the seamline will prevent a seam from growing. This is called staystitching. Overlocking seams or zigzag stitching over raw edges of seams are the quickest seam finishes.

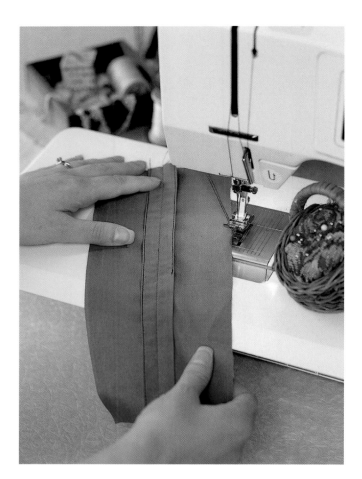

Turned Under Edge: After pressing open the seam, turn under raw edges $1/8$" and stitch close to folded edge.

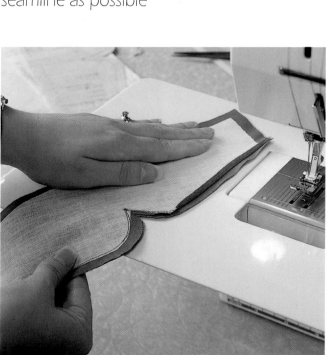

To edge-press a seam, fold open the top seam layer and press it flat.

9. using special seam finishes

Turned Under Edge:

This is a finish to use for an exposed seam that cannot be practically enclosed. Turn raw edges of the seam under $1/8$" and stitch close to the folded edge.

French Seam:

Using a French seam is an excellent and simple way to fully enclose raw seam edges. Pin the seam, wrong sides together, and stitch, taking a $1/4$" seam allowance. Trim seam to $1/8$". Press flat, then press to one side. Pin seam, right sides together, and stitch,

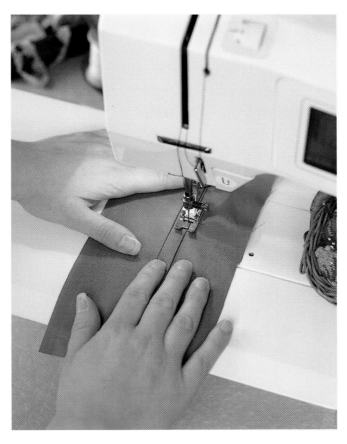

French Seam: Pin trimmed seam, right sides together and stitch, taking a ¹/₄" seam allowance and encasing all raw edges.

Flat Felled or Inside Felled Seam: After trimming lower seam allowance, turn edge of the upper seam allowance under and stitch seam to garment close to the folded edge.

taking a ¹/₄" seam allowance and encasing raw edges. Press flat, then press to one side.

Topstitched Seam:

From the right side, stitch the specified distance from the seam through all fabric thicknesses.

Doublestitched and Overcast Edge Seam:

Stitch a plain seam, then stitch again ¹/₄" from first row. Trim seam close to the second row of stitching. Zigzag-stitch over trimmed edge, then press. This method duplicates the type of seam an overlock sewing machine makes.

Flat Felled or Inside Felled Seam:

Stitch a plain seam and press it toward one side. Trim the lower seam allowance to ¹/₈". Turn the edge of the upper seam allowance under ¹/₄" while machine-stitching close to the folded edge.

Stitch-in-the-Ditch:

The ditch is located just to the outside of a seam. By stitching-in-the-ditch, stitches should be barely visible.

Seaming Bias:

In order to seam bias cuts, the short edges from two bias pieces must be angled identically, and the angle must be along a grain-line. If necessary, trim bias edges to match grainline, then place edges, right sides together, and stitch a ¹/₄" seam. Repeat until all lengths have been seamed. Press seams open. It is not necessary to join the last piece to the first.

To join the bias pieces together, align the bias ends at the seamline and stitch, taking a ¹/₄" seam allowance.

10. making darts

Fold the vest piece, right sides together, along the center dart line.

Horizontally pin the dart, matching dots. Mark the beginning and the ending of the dart with pins. For a visual aid, use a ruler and fabric marking pen to connect the dots and show the shape of the dart. Stitch along the traced line.

For darts with a wide base, begin at the base and taper to nothing at the end of the dart.

For contour shaped darts, begin stitching at the center of the dart, tapering to nothing at each end. For

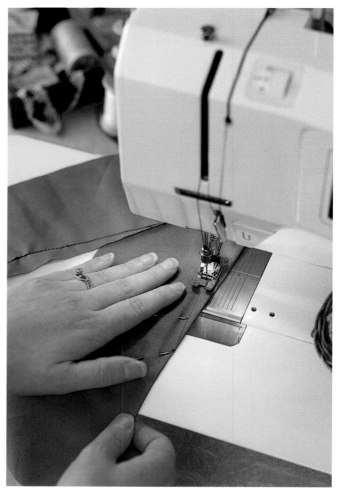

Begin to stitch a contour-shaped dart at the center, tapering stitches at each end.

either dart, gradually decrease stitch size at dart ends to eliminate the need to backstitch. Clip contour darts at the center and along the fold.

Darts are always stitched and pressed first before proceeding with major construction seams.

11. using facings

Shaped Facings:

If indicated on the pattern, stitch facings together. Press seams open. Stitch $^3/_8$" along all outer facing edges unless indicated otherwise on pattern. Clip facing at curves to stitching. Press facing under along stitching. Stitch close to the pressed edge. If preferred, trim facing edge $^1/_8$" past stitching and overcast edges.

After facing has been stitched on the vest edges, trim

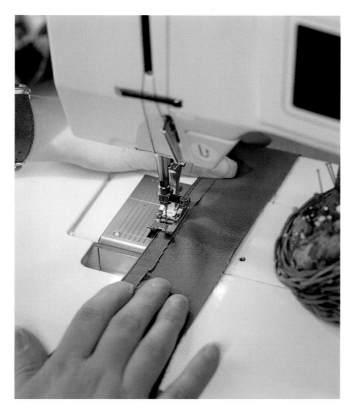

After the facing edge has been turned under, stitch close to the pressed edge.

Understitch opened out facing or lining to the seam allowance.

bulk, grade seam allowances, and clip curves.

Facing seam allowances are always pressed toward the facing. Open out facing and understitch it to the seam allowance. This will prevent facing from rolling to the outside.

Turn facing to inside and press. Loosely tack facing to garment at seams or topstitch the entire facing to garment for a sportswear finish.

Bias Facings:

Cut bias tape 2" longer than the area to be stitched. Open out prepackaged bias tape and press open. Fold in half, matching long edges, and press. If garment edge is curved, steam press the bias tape into a curved shape.

EAU CLAIRE DISTRICT LIBRARY

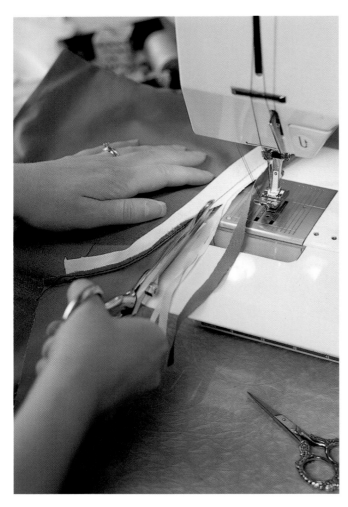

Trim bias seam to 1/4". Press seam toward bias.

Understitch as for a shaped facing. Turn bias to the inside and topstitch bias facing in place.

12. using bias bindings

Cut bias as specified for vest and seam together.

Press seams open. Before stitching bias in place, steam press the length of the bias while stretching it slightly. Cut bias 2" longer than the garment edge to be bound. Beginning at an inconspicuous seam, and beginning to stitch 3/4" away from that

Join bias ends on mark and press open.

Stitch the raw edges of the bias tape to the garment edge, right sides together. Beginning at an inconspicuous seam, and beginning to stitch 3/4" away from that seam, stitch the bias facing to the garment edge (such as an armhole), taking a 1/2" seam. Make certain to leave a 1/2" seam allowance on bias at the ends. End stitching 3/4" from the seam. Align bias ends to side seam and mark. Stitch bias ends together on mark. Trim seam to 3/8" and press open. Complete stitching bias to garment. Press seam toward bias.

seam, stitch the bias to the garment edge (such as an armhole), taking a $1/2$" seam. Make certain to leave a $1/2$" seam allowance on bias at the ends. End stitching $3/4$" from the seam. Align bias ends to side seam and mark. Stitch bias ends together on mark. Trim seam to $3/8$" and press open. Complete bias seam.

Trim seam to $1/4$", press seam toward bias. Turn under remaining edge of bias while folding bias over garment seam to encase. Pin, so the turned under edge is placed just beyond the seam and so heads of pins face the outward folded edge of the bias.

Edgestitch bias from right side of garment just to the inside of the seam, through all thicknesses, and catching in turned under edge on wrong side of garment. Remove pins while stitching. Press.

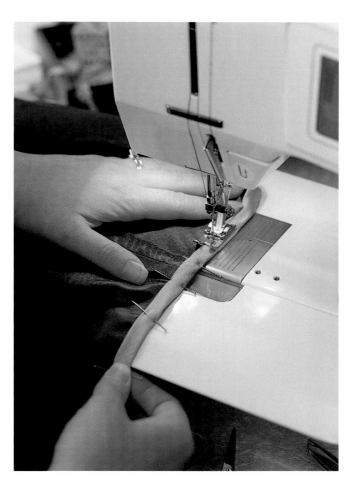

Stitch bias from right side of garment, directly to the right of the seam, catching in turned under edge while stitching.

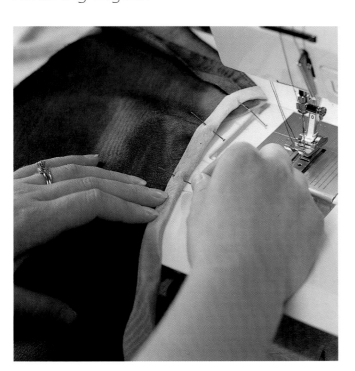

Face heads of pins toward the outward folded edge of bias binding.

13. making collars

Trim the collar interfacing pieces so there is a $1/8$" seam allowance on all edges. Make certain to trim the interfacing flush to the corner point seamline. According to manufacturer's directions, fuse in place.

For a nicely shaped collar, trim $1/8$" from outer (un-notched) edges of remaining collar piece. This becomes the under-collar. Pin top collar to undercollar, right sides together or as specified in the individual vest instructions. Stitch, taking a $3/8$" seam allowance, easing undercollar to fit top collar. Remember to take one or two stitches across collar points. Doublestitch 1" along seam on either side of a point. Do not stitch neck edge.

Grade seam allowances, trim bulk from points, and clip curves if applicable. Edge-press as much of collar as possible before turning right side out.

Use a pointer and creaser or a pin to coax the collar point out. Press collar from the underside. Align and baste-stitch neck edges together.

Grade seam allowances and trim bulk from collar points.

Fuse trimmed interfacing to collar.

After coaxing out collar points, press collar from the underside.

14. making pockets

Lined Pockets:

When lining pockets, stitch pocket lining to the pocket, right sides together, matching notched edges. Press seam open.

Fold pocket over on foldline, right sides together. Stitch sides and lower edges, taking a $3/8$" seam allowance or as specified in the individual vest instructions. Do not stitch across folded edge. Trim bulk from corners and clip curves. Edge-press seams. Cut a slit in the pocket lining near the bottom edge to pull pocket right side out through the opening. Press pocket flat. Fuse a small piece of interfacing over the slit in the lining.

Pin pocket in place on vest front and topstitch.

Fake Welt Pockets & Pocket Flaps:

When making fake welt pockets, fold the fake welt pocket in half, matching notched edges, and press along the fold. On wrong side, fuse bias interfacing to half of the fake welt pocket, beginning $1/8$" past the center fold.

Fold welt, right sides together, and stitch short ends, taking a $3/8$" seam or as specified in the individual vest instructions. Trim bulk from corners and edge-press. Turn right side out. Press welts from the underside.

Pin fake welt to vest front, right sides together, having raw edge of welt $1/2$" above line indicated. Stitch $1/2$" from edge. Trim seam allowance to $1/4$".

Press welt upward, covering raw

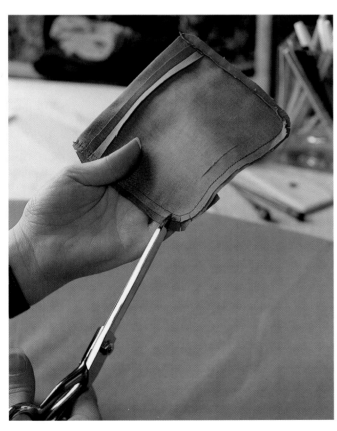

Cut slit in pocket lining near bottom edge. Trim bulk from corners and clip curves.

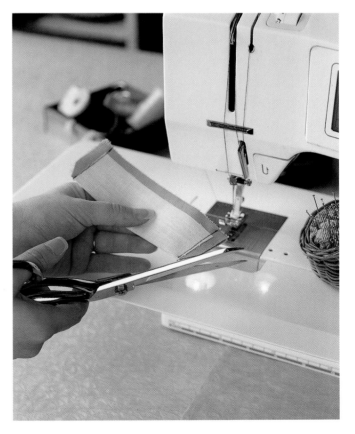

Stitch folded fake welt pocket at short ends, taking a $3/8$" seam allowance. Trim corners.

edges, and machine- or hand-stitch ends of welt to vest front.

Approach and stitch pocket flaps and belts similar to collars. Pin pocket flap to vest front, right sides together, having raw edge of flap $1/2$" below line indicated. Stitch $1/2$" from edge. Trim seam allowance to $3/16$".

Press flap downward, covering raw edges, and top-stitch $1/4$" from seam.

15. making a buttonhole

It may not be possible to find the right button for the vest in the size indicated in the list of materials. Buttonhole lengths should be made $1/8$" longer than the diameter of the button.

Most sewing machines have a pre-scribed method for stitching button-holes to their best advantage. Like-wise, your sewing machine may have an automatic buttonholer.

In either case, follow the manual's methods.

For buttonholes that will be stitched on lightweight or a single layer of

Pin fake welt pocket to vest front, having raw edges of welt $1/2$" above pocket placement line.

Use masking tape as a guide for stitching equally-sized buttonholes.

fabric, stabilize the buttonhole area by fusing a small piece of interfacing to the wrong side of the fabric.

To help make all the buttonholes equal in size, cut two pieces of masking or machine-basting tape to the exact buttonhole size. Place the tape equidistant from buttonhole center and so the center space is $^5/_{16}$".

Use the tape as a stitch length guide and satin-stitch buttonhole according to the method prescribed for your sewing machine.

Use buttonhole scissors or a utility knife to cut through center of buttonhole. Do not cut across bar tack at ends.

Whip-stitch buttonholes with contrasting or matching 4mm silk ribbon

for an elegant, but simple finish. Invisibly begin and end ribbon on the underside of the garment.

When making chainstitched thread loops, use quadrupled thread. Securely fasten the thread to the garment with two small overlapping stitches. Form a loop by taking another short stitch over the previous stitches. Slip a loop of remaining thread through the first loop and grab it with the other hand. Tighten the first loop around the second and continue in this manner until you have the specified chainstitched length. Stitch the needle through the loop to complete. Stitch the bottom end of the loop in place and secure with several small stitches.

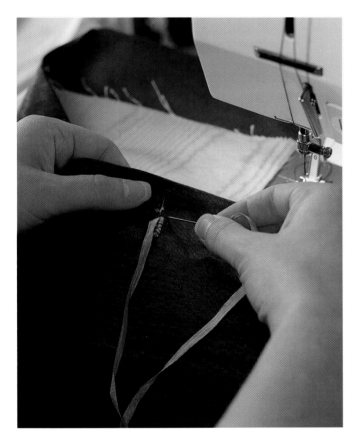

Whipstitch 4mm silk ribbon over buttonholes for an elegant, simple finish.

16. assembling a vest

Fusing Bias Cut Interfacing Strips:

After the front edge interfacing piece has been trimmed and fused in place, fuse the bias interfacing strips to the remaining bottom edges of the front, placing interfacing $^3/_8$" in from cut edges and seam edges. Fuse interfacing to the back in the same manner.

Refer to the "now and forever" vest on pages 79-94.

Vest Lining:

After vest fronts and back and lining fronts and back have been stitched together at the shoulders, pin the lining to the vest, right sides together, matching front edge notches, shoulder, and center back neck seams and armhole edges. Stitch back neck, vest front, and armhole edges, taking a $^1/_2$" seam allowance.

Fuse bias interfacing strip to vest front, $3/8$" in from bottom edges.

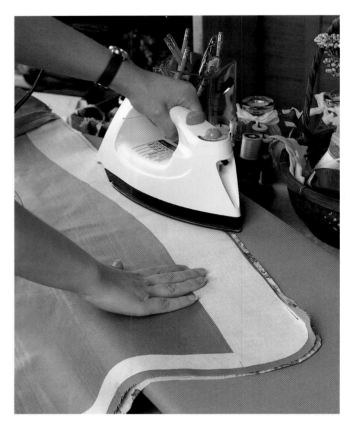

Edge-press all vest seams.

Pin and stitch vest to vest lining, right sides together.

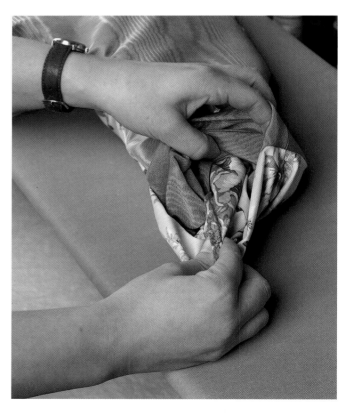

Turn vest right side out by pulling front through shoulders toward the back.

Trim bulk from corners, grade seam allowances, and clip curves. Edge-press all seams.

Turn right side out, pulling front through shoulders toward back. It may be helpful to understitch back and front vest neck edges now.

Vest Side Seams & Lower Edge:

Pin and stitch vest front to back at side seams, matching notches and armhole seams, taking a $1/2$" seam. In a continuous seam from outer fabric, pin and stitch lining front to back at side seams. Leave a $4^1/2$" opening at one lining side seam. Press side seams open.

Pin and stitch the lower edge of the vest to the vest lining, right sides together, matching seams, taking a $1/2$" seam allowance and breaking stitch at center back dot if indicated on pattern. Trim bulk from corners, grade seam allowances, and clip curves. Edge-press lower vest seam.

Turn vest right side out through the lining side seam opening and press vest thoroughly.

Stitch lower vest edge.

Turn vest right side out through lining side seam opening.

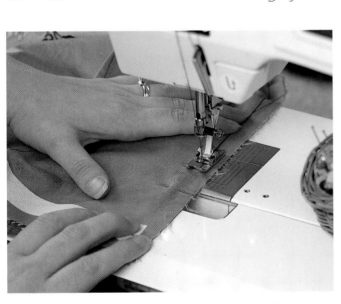

Stitch front to back at side seams. In a continuous seam from outer fabric, stitch lining front to back at side seams.

collars &
pockets

making a shawl collar

Patterns for this collar can be found with the accompanying vests.

Each top side of a collar has one left and one right piece. Each underside of a collar has a matching left and right piece. Outer collar edge has a $1/2$" seam allowance.

Trim the shawl collar interfacing pieces so there is a $1/8$" seam allowance on all edges.

Fuse interfacing to wrong side of one left and one right collar. Interfacing designates collar pieces as "top." According to manufacturer's directions, fuse in place.

For a nicely shaped collar, trim $1/8$" from outer (unnotched) edges of undercollar pieces. Pin top collar to undercollar, wrong sides together. Baste-stitch $3/8$" from edge.

Press bias strip with iron while stretching it gently. Stitch right side of bias to outer edge of collar top side, taking a $1/2$" seam allowance. Trim seam to $1/4$". Press seam toward binding.

Turn under remaining edge of bias while folding bias over collar edge to enclose. Pin so folded under edge is placed $1/8$" beyond seam and so heads of pins face outward. Stitch bias in-the-ditch, catching folded under bias edge while stitching. Press.

Align and pin collar neck edges, baste-stitch $3/8$" from edge. Top collar is slightly larger than undercollar.

Stitch collar to vest neck edges as specified in the individual vest instructions.

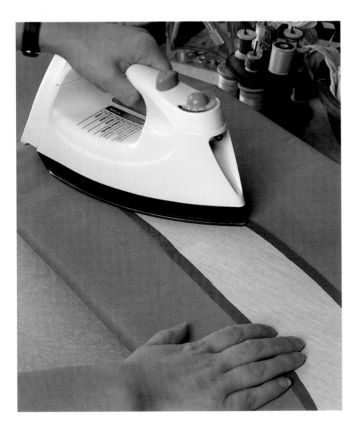

Fuse trimmed interfacing to collar pieces. Interfacing designates a collar piece at "top."

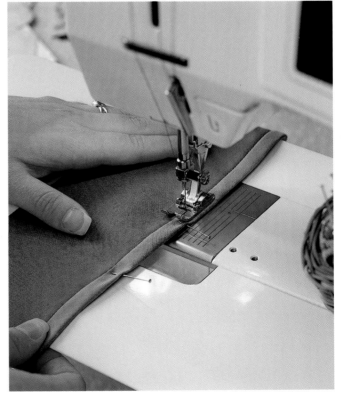

Stitch directly to the left of bias binding seam to "stitch-in-the-ditch."

making a soft-notch collar

Patterns for this collar can be found with the accompanying vests.

Each top side of a collar has one left and one right piece. Each underside of a collar has a matching left and right piece. Outer collar edge has a ³/₈" seam allowance.

Trim the soft-notch collar inter-facing pieces so there is a ¹/₈" seam allowance on all edges.

Fuse interfacing to wrong side of one left and one right collar. Inter-facing designates collar pieces as "top." According to manufacturer's directions, fuse in place.

For a nicely shaped collar, trim ¹/₈" from outer (un-notched) edges of undercollar pieces. Pin top collar to undercollar, right sides together, eas-ing undercollar to fit top collar. Stitch all outer edges, taking a ³/₈" seam allowance and easing edges to fit. Doublestitch a 1" section at inward, soft-notch point. Do not stitch neck or shoulder edges.

Grade seam allowances, clip curves, and clip to inward soft-notch point. Edge-press.

Turn right side out, press from the underside. Use a pointer and creaser or a pin to coax out collar curves. Press collar from the underside.

Align and pin collar neck edges, baste-stitch ³/₈" from edge. Top collar is slightly larger than under-collar.

Stitch collar to vest neck edges as specified in the individual vest instructions.

Doublestitch a 1" section of inward point on the soft-notch collar, directly to the right of the first row of stitching.

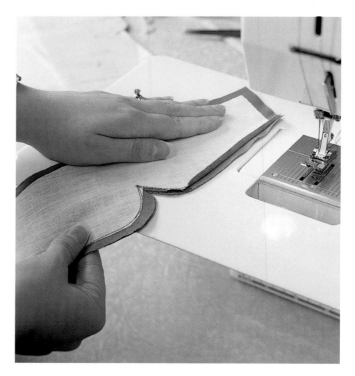

Clip to inward soft-notch collar point. Edge-press before turning right side out.

making a notch collar

Patterns for this collar can be found with the accompanying vests.

Collar pieces include two left and two right collar lapels, two collars, one left and one right collar lapel interfacing piece, and one collar interfacing piece. Outer collar edge has a 3/8" seam allowance.

Trim the collar lapel and the collar interfacing pieces so there is a 1/8" seam allowance on all edges. Make certain to trim interfacing flush to corner point seamline.

Fuse interfacing to wrong side of one left and one right collar lapel and to collar. Interfacing designates collar pieces as "top." According to manufacturer's directions, fuse in place.

For a nicely shaped collar, trim 1/8" from outer (unnotched) edges of undercollar and undercollar lapel pieces. Stitch top collar to top collar lapels, matching notches and stitching to dot. Stitch undercollar to undercollar lapels, matching notches and stitching to dot. Press seams open.

Pin assembled top collar to assembled undercollar, right sides together. Stitch all outer edges, taking a 3/8" seam allowance and easing undercollar to fit top collar. Break stitches at dot. Remember to take one or two stitches across collar points. Doublestitch 1" along seam on either side of a point. Do not stitch neck edge.

Grade seam allowances, clip curves, and clip to dots. Edge-press.

Turn right side out, press from the underside. Use a pointer and creaser or a pin to coax the collar point out. Press collar from the underside. Align and pin collar neck edges, easing to fit. Baste-stitch 3/8" from edge.

Stitch collar to vest neck edges as specified in the individual vest instructions.

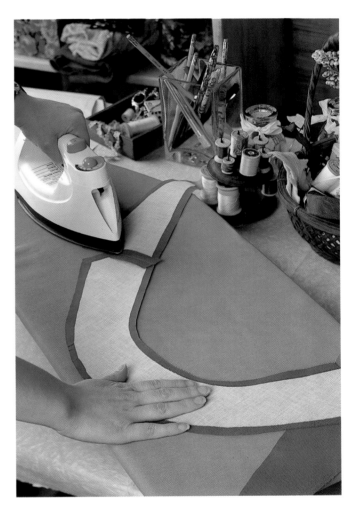

After seaming the notched collar pieces to the collar, press the seam open. Make certain to stitch to dots only at the notched edge.

making a shirt collar

Patterns for this collar can be found with the accompanying vests.

Collar pieces include one top and one undercollar and one collar interfacing piece. Outer collar edge has a $^3/_8$" seam allowance.

Trim the shirt collar interfacing pieces so there is a $^1/_8$" seam allowance on all edges. Make certain to trim the interfacing flush to the corner point seamline. Interfacing designates collar pieces as "top." According to manufacturer's directions, fuse in place.

For a nicely shaped collar, trim $^1/_8$" from outer (unnotched) edges of collar. This becomes the underside of the collar. Pin top collar to undercollar, right sides together. Stitch, taking a $^3/_8$" seam allowance, easing undercollar to fit top collar. Remember to take one or two stitches across collar points. Doublestitch 1" along seam on either side of a point. Do not stitch neck edge.

Trim bulk from points, grade seam allowances, and clip curves if applicable. Edge-press as much of collar as possible before turning right side out.

Use a pointer and creaser or a pin to coax the collar point out. Press collar from the underside. Align and baste-stitch neck edges together.

Stitch collar to vest neck edges as specified in the individual vest instructions.

Fuse trimmed interfacing to collar according to manufacturer's directions.

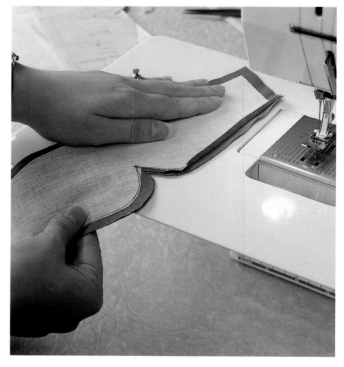

Edge-press as much of collar as possible before turning right side out.

making a squared-off shawl collar

Patterns for this collar can be found with the accompanying vests.

Each top side of a collar has one left and one right piece. Each underside of a collar has a matching left and right piece. Outer collar edge has a ³/₈" seam allowance.

Trim the squared-off shawl collar interfacing pieces so there is a ¹/₈" seam allowance on all edges. Make certain to trim the interfacing flush to the corner point seamline.

Fuse interfacing to wrong side of one left and one right collar. Interfacing designates collar pieces as "top." According to manufacturer's directions, fuse in place.

Mark ⁷/₈" from outer, long edge of interfaced collar. Stitch ribbon over marked line along one selvage edge of ribbon. Press.

For a nicely shaped collar, trim ¹/₈" from outer (un-notched) edges of undercollar pieces. Pin top collar to undercollar, wrong sides together. Stitch all outer edges, taking a ³/₈" seam allowance and easing edges to fit.

Remember to take one or two stitches across collar points. Doublestitch 1" along seam on either side of a point. Do not stitch neck edge.

Grade seam allowances, trim bulk from points, and clip curves if applicable. Edge-press as much of collar as possible before turning right side out.

Use a pointer and creaser or a pin to coax the collar point out. Press collar from the underside. Align and baste-stitch neck edges together.

Stitch collar to vest neck edges as specified in the individual vest instructions.

Stitch edge of ribbon to collar on marked line.

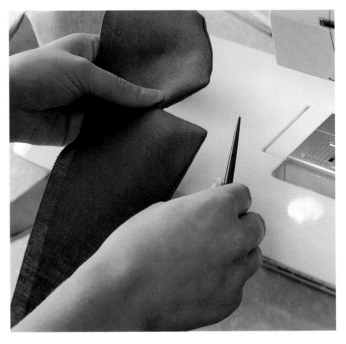

Use a pointer and creaser to coax collar point out.

making a sailor collar

Patterns for this collar can be found with the accompanying vests.

A sailor collar can be single or double layered.

For a double layered sailor collar, cut two from collar pattern and cut one from interfacing.

Trim the sailor collar interfacing piece so there is a $1/8$" seam allowance on all edges. Make certain to trim the interfacing flush to the corner point seamline.

According to manufacturer's directions, fuse in place.

Stitch, trim, and press according to instructions for making a shirt collar on page 26.

For a lace-embellished collar that has a single layer, begin with the corner of a hanky at the center back of the collar to collage lace trims and appliqués onto the right side of the collar fabric. When pleased with the arrangement, use a narrow zigzag stitch to machine-stitch laces in place.

To finish the edge of the collar, stitch right side of $3/4$"-wide lace trim to the right side of the outer edges of the collar, taking a $1/4$" seam allowance and pleating lace at the back corners.

Stitch again directly to the right of the first row of stitching. Trim the seam close to the second stitched row. Zigzag-stitch over the narrow seam. Press lace seam toward the collar.

Stitch collar to vest neck edges as specified in the individual vest instructions.

When pleased with arrangement, use a narrow machine zigzag stitch to stitch laces in place.

Stitch edge of $3/4$"-wide lace trim to collar edge, taking a $1/4$" seam allowance.

stitching pockets to vest using a blanket stitch

Hem and prepare pocket according to instructions on pages 30-31.

Pin pocket in place on vest front.

Use six strands of embroidery floss to hand-stitch pocket to vest front with the blanket stitch.

Beginning at the top right corner, bring floss to front at outer edge of pocket. Stitch back into pocket/vest front $1/4$" into the pocket, but spaced $1/8$" from entry point. Bring the needle back up at outer edge of pocket $1/8$" from entry point.

Loop thread under needle and pull floss through fabric.

Repeat stitching until pocket is attached to vest front.

making a fake welt pocket

Patterns for this pocket can be found on pages 32-33. This pocket can be used on any vest as desired.

When making fake welt pockets, fold the fake welt pocket in half, matching notched edges, and press along the fold. On wrong side, fuse bias interfacing to half of the fake welt pocket, beginning $1/8$" past the center fold.

Trim bulk from fake welt pocket corners, then edge-press the seam.

Fold welt, right sides together, and stitch short ends, taking a $3/8$" seam or as specified in the individual vest instructions. Trim bulk from corners and edge-press. Turn right side out. Press welts from the underside.

Pin fake welt to vest front, right sides together, having raw edge of welt $1/2$" above line indicated. Stitch $1/2$" from edge. Trim seam allowance to $1/4$".

Press welt upward, covering raw edges, and machine or hand-stitch ends of welt to vest front.

Stitch fake welt to vest front, taking a $1/2$" seam allowance.

making a standard patch pocket

Patterns for this pocket can be found on pages 32-33. This pocket can be used on any vest as desired.

A patch pocket can be made with the same fabric as the vest or with contrasting fabric and can be made in just about any size and shape imaginable. In addition, patch pockets can be lined or remain unlined.

Patch pockets are topstitched to the outside of a garment.

The most important thing to remember when placing pockets is to get them evenly placed, matching the pocket placement on the right and left vest fronts.

When unlined patch pockets are desired, see "making a pleated patch pocket".

When lined patch pockets are desired, see "Lined Pockets" on page 17.

For a lined patch pocket, clip curves, then turn the pocket right side out through the slit in the lining.

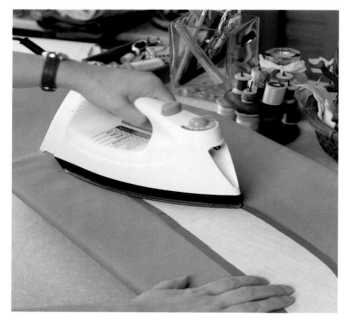

Fuse a small piece of interfacing over slit in pocket lining.

making a pleated patch pocket

Patterns for this pocket can be found on pages 32-33. This pocket can be used on any vest as desired.

Fuse a strip of $3/4$"-wide bias cut interfacing to the underside of the pleated pocket, $1/8$" above the foldline. To create the pocket hem, press under $1/4$" along the top edge of the pleated pocket. Fold the top of the pleated pocket over on the foldline, to the right side of the fabric.

Stitch the ends, beginning at fold and continue stitching along pocket raw edges at a $3/8$" seam allowance.

Trim corners and clip curves. Turn the top fold, right side out, and press. Press under remain-

Stitch 3/8" in from side and lower pocket edges while also stitching pocket hem.

Fold pressed edge of pocket to pocket center forming an inverted box pleat.

Press pocket edges under to wrong side along stitching.

ing pocket seam allowance along the stitching.

On the wrong side of the pleated pocket, fold and press the fabric along the left foldline. Fold the pressed edge to the center of pleated pocket. Press, forming half of an inverted box pleat. On the wrong side, fold and press the fabric along the right foldline. Fold the pressed edge to the center of pleated pocket. Press, forming remainder of inverted box pleat. Pin in place.

Topstitch close to the top and bottom edges of the pocket hem.

Stitch pocket to vest as specified in the individual vest instructions.

binding a patch pocket with bias

To create pocket hem, press under 1/4" along the top edge of the pocket. Fold the top of the pocket over on the foldline, to the inside of the fabric. Stitch hem in place.

Press bias strip with an iron while gently stretching it. Stitch the bias to the outer edge of the pocket, right sides together, taking a $^1/_2$" seam allowance and extending the bias $^1/_2$" past the fin-ished pocket edge. Do not stitch the bias to the top folded edge of the pocket.

Trim seam to $^3/_{16}$". Press seam toward the binding.

Turn under the remaining edge of the bias while folding the bias over the pocket seam to enclose it and turn the bias under at top pocket edge for a clean finish. Pin so the folded under edges are placed just be-yond the seam.

Stitch pocket to vest as specified in the individual vest instructions.

Turn bias under at top pocket edge for a clean finish.

enlarge all patterns 285%

LARGE POCKET FLAP
cut 2 from fabric
for each side and
cut 1 from interfacing
for each side

grainline

LINING

grainline

ROUNDED PATCH POCKET

LINING
cut 1 from
lining fabric
for each side

POCKET
cut 1 from
fabric
for each side

use $^3/_8$" seam allowance around edges and $^1/_4$" seam allowance across top

POCKET

grainline

Stitch bias strip to pocket edge, taking a $^3/_8$" seam allowance and clipping bias at curves.

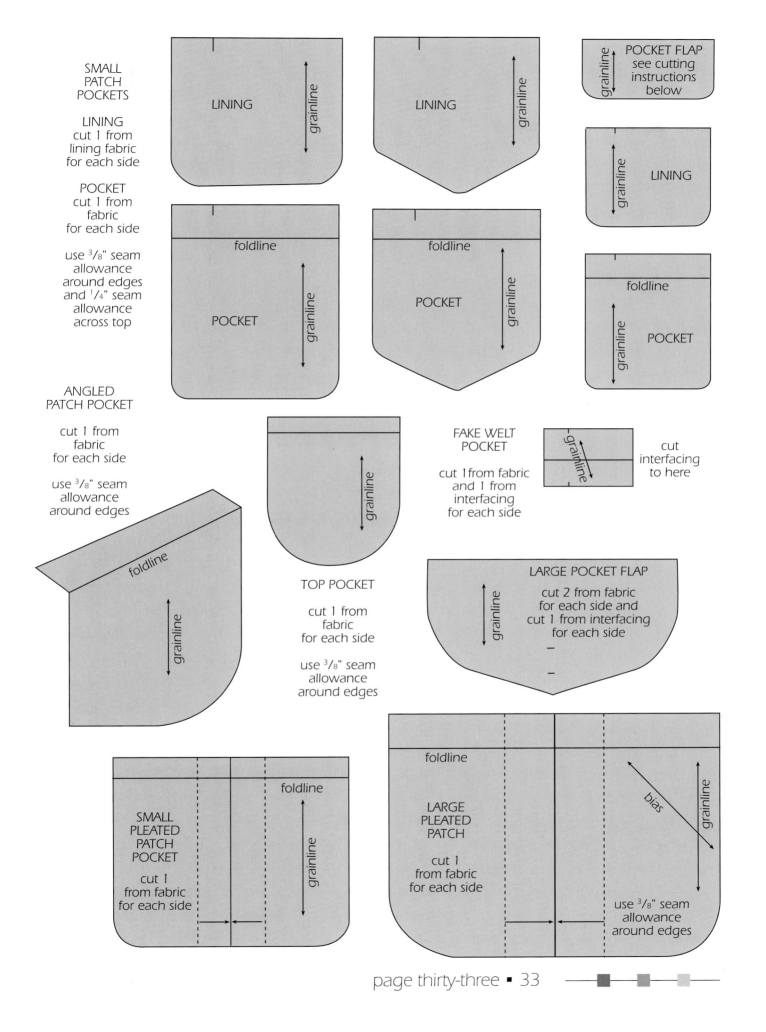

SMALL
PATCH
POCKETS

LINING
cut 1 from
lining fabric
for each side

POCKET
cut 1 from
fabric
for each side

use $^3/_8$" seam
allowance
around edges
and $^1/_4$" seam
allowance
across top

ANGLED
PATCH POCKET

cut 1 from
fabric
for each side

use $^3/_8$" seam
allowance
around edges

LINING

grainline

LINING

grainline

POCKET FLAP
see cutting
instructions
below

grainline

LINING

grainline

foldline

POCKET

grainline

foldline

POCKET

grainline

foldline

POCKET

grainline

foldline

grainline

grainline

TOP POCKET

cut 1 from
fabric
for each side

use $^3/_8$" seam
allowance
around edges

FAKE WELT
POCKET

cut 1 from fabric
and 1 from
interfacing
for each side

grainline

cut
interfacing
to here

LARGE POCKET FLAP

cut 2 from fabric
for each side and
cut 1 from interfacing
for each side

grainline

SMALL
PLEATED
PATCH
POCKET

cut 1
from fabric
for each side

foldline

grainline

foldline

LARGE
PLEATED
PATCH

cut 1
from fabric
for each side

bias

grainline

use $^3/_8$" seam
allowance
around edges

breath of
fresh air . . .
the basic vest

breath of fresh air

Small talk
smothers you.
You prefer
quiet company.
Soft and simple
contemplation
by the fire.
To all who love you,
your serenity
and ease are a
breath of fresh air.
This vest speaks softly
of the comfort you desire.

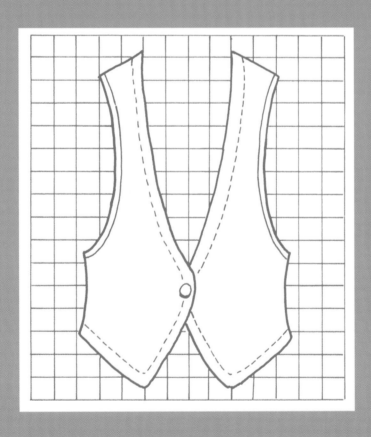

breath of
fresh air . . .
the basic vest

breath of fresh air

materials needed

fabric one:
  44"-wide,
    1 1/4 yard
  54"- to 60"-wide,
    1 yard
lining:
  44"- to 60"-wide,
    7/8 yard
fusible interfacing:
  18"-wide,
    3/8 yard
button:
  decorative

IMPORTANT:

- Before beginning, it is recommended that you carefully read "learning the basics" on pages 5-21 and "collars & pockets" on pages 22-33.

- Yardages have been calculated for making the basic vest in a medium size. Adjust yardage amounts accordingly for collars, pockets, and variations in size or fabric usage.

1. cutting fabrics

fabric one:
  front, cut 2
  back, cut 1
    along fold
  back facing,
    cut 1 along fold
  pleat stay,
    cut 1
  armhole binding,
    cut 2"-wide
      bias strips, 64"
lining:
  front, cut 2
fusible interfacing:
  cut 1"-wide
    bias strips, 74"

- For armhole binding, cut enough bias strips for a total of 64" in length and seam together.

- For fusible interfacing, cut enough bias strips for a total of 74" in length, but do not seam together.

- Transfer all markings from pattern to vest pieces.

- Stitch vest in an assembly line manner for speedier results.

2. preparing vest pieces

Press back hem up 3/4" to wrong side. Turn raw edge under 1/4" and stitch hem in place.

On the right side of the back, fold and press the fabric along the left fold-line. Fold the pressed edge to the center of back. Press, forming half of box pleat. Fold and press the fabric along the right foldline and fold to the center. Press, forming remainder of box pleat. Pin in place 4" up from hem edge.

On pleat stay, turn under 1/4" along one short edge to wrong side and press. Fold, right sides together, matching longer edges. Stitch 1/4" seam. Finger-press seam open. Place the seam at the center of the piece and stitch along the bottom edge, taking a 1/4" seam allowance. Trim corners. Turn right side out and press.

Pin the pleat stay in place over the box pleat where indicated on pattern. Topstitch in place.

Fuse bias interfacing strips to wrong side of the fronts, placing the interfacing 3/8" in from the cut edge along the neck and bottom edges. Fuse interfacing to the back neck edge in the same manner.

When adding a collar, trim collar interfacing pieces so there is a $1/8$" seam allowance on all edges. Fuse interfacing to the wrong sides of collar pieces.

Prepare collar at this time according to instructions on pages 23-28.

When adding pockets, fuse the interfacing to the wrong side of the pocket pieces.

Prepare pockets at this time according to instructions on pages 29-32.

3. stitching beginning vest elements

Follow instructions on pages 29-32 to add fake welt or patch pockets to vest fronts.

When adding a squared-off shawl collar, pin assembled collar to front neck edge and shoulders, matching notches. Baste-stitch having collar underside

against right side of front.

Stitch fronts to back at shoulder seam and side seams, right sides together, taking a $1/2$" seam allowance. Press seams toward front and topstitch.

When adding a sailor collar, pin assembled collar to front and back neck edges, matching notches and shoulder marks. Baste-stitch having collar underside against right side of front and back.

4. stitching lining & back neck facing to vest

Stitch $3/8$" along the outer edge of back neck facing. Clip to stitching. Press facing edge under along stitching and edgestitch.

Stitch back neck facing to the left and the right front lining, right sides together, at the shoulders, taking a $1/2$" seam

allowance. Press seam open, pressing the remaining, unstitched portion of the shoulder seam under as well.

Pin lining and back neck facing to vest, right sides together, matching shoulder seams and all front edges.

Stitch facing and lining to back neck and all front edges up to side seams, taking a $1/2$" seam allowance.

Cut bulk from corners, grade seam allowances, and clip curves.

Edge-press neck and bottom edges. Turn right side out. Lining is not stitched at the side seams at this time.

Press back and front vest neck edges toward the lining and back neck facing.

Understitch front and back neck edges. Stitch as far down the vest front as possible.

Turn lining side seams under $1/2$". Pin the lining side seams

in place over the vest side seams, wrong sides together. Machine- or hand-stitch the lining to the side seams. Press thoroughly.

Pin the lining in place at the shoulder, enclosing the shoulder seam.

Pin the facing to the back neck. Machine- or hand-stitch the facing to shoulder seams.

When bias binding the back neck and vest front edges, eliminate step 4. Bind vest edges following instructions in step 6.

5. topstitching vest front & back neck

When topstitching is desired, measure and mark vest front $3/4$" from edges and stitch through all thicknesses on marks.

For some vest styles, you will find it helpful to topstitch as close to vest edges as possible, including underneath a collar when applicable.

6. binding armholes with bias

If vest is to be lined, pin lining to vest at armholes. Using bias fabric and beginning at side seam, stitch bias to armhole, taking a $1/2$" seam allowance. Leave a $1/2$" seam allowance on bias at side seam and begin stitches $3/4$" away from side seam. End stitching $3/4$" prior to side seam.

Align bias ends to side seam and mark. Stitch bias ends together on mark. Trim seam to $3/8$" and press open. Finish stitching bias to armhole at side seam. Trim seam to $1/4$". Press seam toward binding. Turn under the remaining edge of the bias while folding the bias over armhole seam to enclose. Pin it so the folded under edge is placed just beyond the seam and so the heads of the pins face the armhole opening. Edgestitch the bias from the right side just to the inside of the seam, catching in folded over edge on the underside. Remove the pins while stitching.

7. finishing

Press vest again thoroughly, using a moistened press cloth, if necessary.

Mark and stitch a single buttonhole on right front. Stitch a button in place on left front.

the basic vest . . .

Actual vest shown on pages 34 & 36

This single-buttoned vest with bias binding around the armholes is a casual vest that can be transformed to elegant by the fabric you choose, by the blouse that it is worn with, and by the embellishments that are chosen. Topstitching is used to accentuate the vest front edges.

The sample vest was made from the following materials:
Fabric one: cotton twill stripe fabric, brown with black stripe
Lining: satin, black
Decorative button: brown

. . . with a
seamed front
& bias-bound
edges

. . . with a seamed front & bias-bound edges

Seaming the front of this vest is a wonderful way to add country charm. Bias binding around all outside edges, including the armholes, back neck, and all front edges, can be done with coordinating or contrasting fabrics for two different looks that are both very effective.

For armhole and collar binding, cut enough bias strips for the total length and seam together.

The sample vest was made from the following materials:
Fabric one: cotton toweling fabric, white with blue stripes
Fabric two: linen kitchen towel, blue/white
Front overlay: men's hanky, navy/gray/cream
Decorative button: blue

Actual vest shown on page 40

...adding a
squared-off
shawl collar

. . . adding a
squared-off
shawl collar

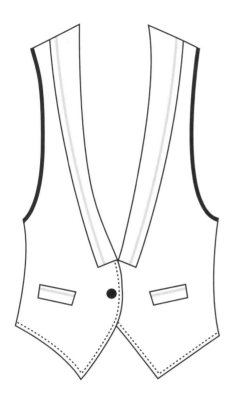

Adding a squared-off shawl collar
gives this vest a richness that would
fit the wardrobe of any executive. The
collar ends at the shoulders. To soften
the sharp edges of the collar and
fake welt pockets, velvet ribbon trim was
added. The fabric chosen in deep, rich tones
also enhances the vest. Bias binding around
the armholes gives a nice finish.

The sample vest was made from the following
materials:
Fabric one: jacquard, burgundy/beige
Fabric two: moiré faille, beige
Lining: crepe de chine, beige
Ribbon trim: velvet, burgundy
Decorative button: antique brass

Actual vest shown on page 42

. . . adding
rounded
patch
pockets

. . . adding rounded patch pockets

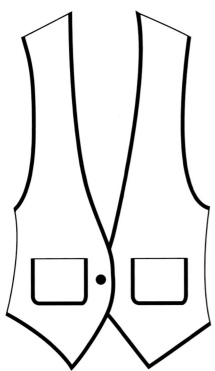

Back to the basics! The basic vest was made with contemporary-looking fabric to assure the wearer that she is confident and up-to-date on fashion issues. The rounded patch pockets have been bound with bias that matches the bias used around the armholes and outside edges of the vest.

For armhole, collar, and pocket binding cut enough bias strips for the total length and seam together.

The sample vest was made from the following materials:
   Fabric one: cotton fabric, mushroom/black print
   Fabric two: tweed, gray/brown/black
   Bias binding: satin, black
   Decorative button: dark mother of pearl

Actual vest shown on page 44

. . . adding a
sailor collar

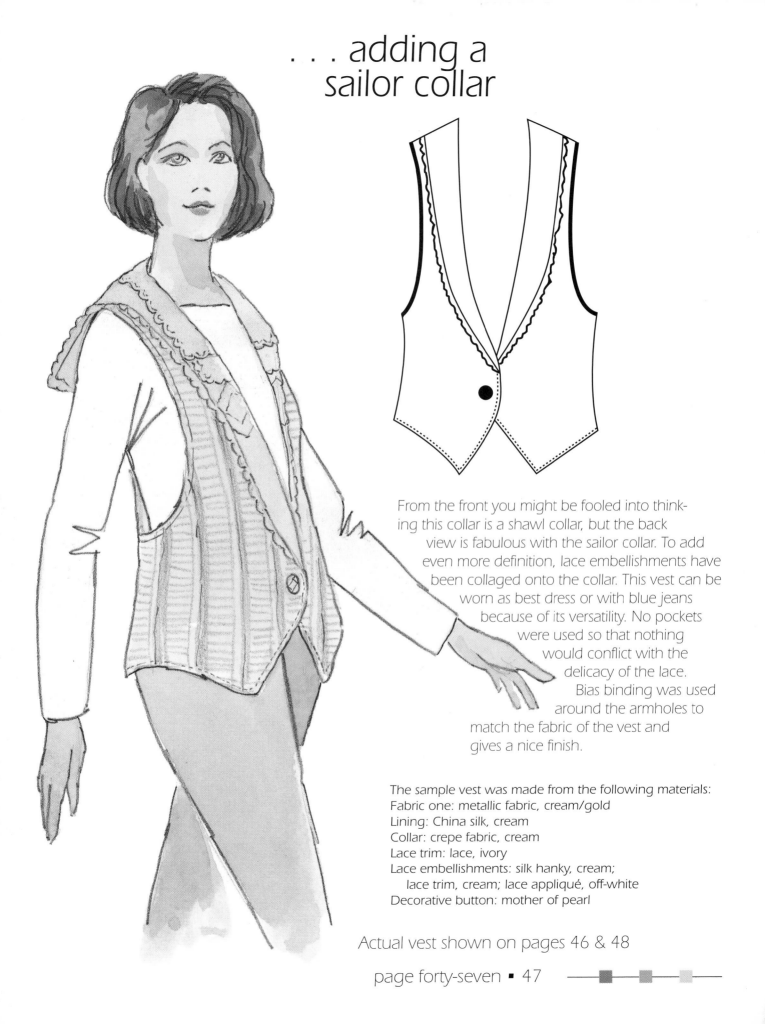

From the front you might be fooled into think-
ing this collar is a shawl collar, but the back
view is fabulous with the sailor collar. To add
even more definition, lace embellishments have
been collaged onto the collar. This vest can be
worn as best dress or with blue jeans
because of its versatility. No pockets
were used so that nothing
would conflict with the
delicacy of the lace.
Bias binding was used
around the armholes to
match the fabric of the vest and
gives a nice finish.

The sample vest was made from the following materials:
Fabric one: metallic fabric, cream/gold
Lining: China silk, cream
Collar: crepe fabric, cream
Lace trim: lace, ivory
Lace embellishments: silk hanky, cream;
    lace trim, cream; lace appliqué, off-white
Decorative button: mother of pearl

Actual vest shown on pages 46 & 48

. . . adding a
sailor collar

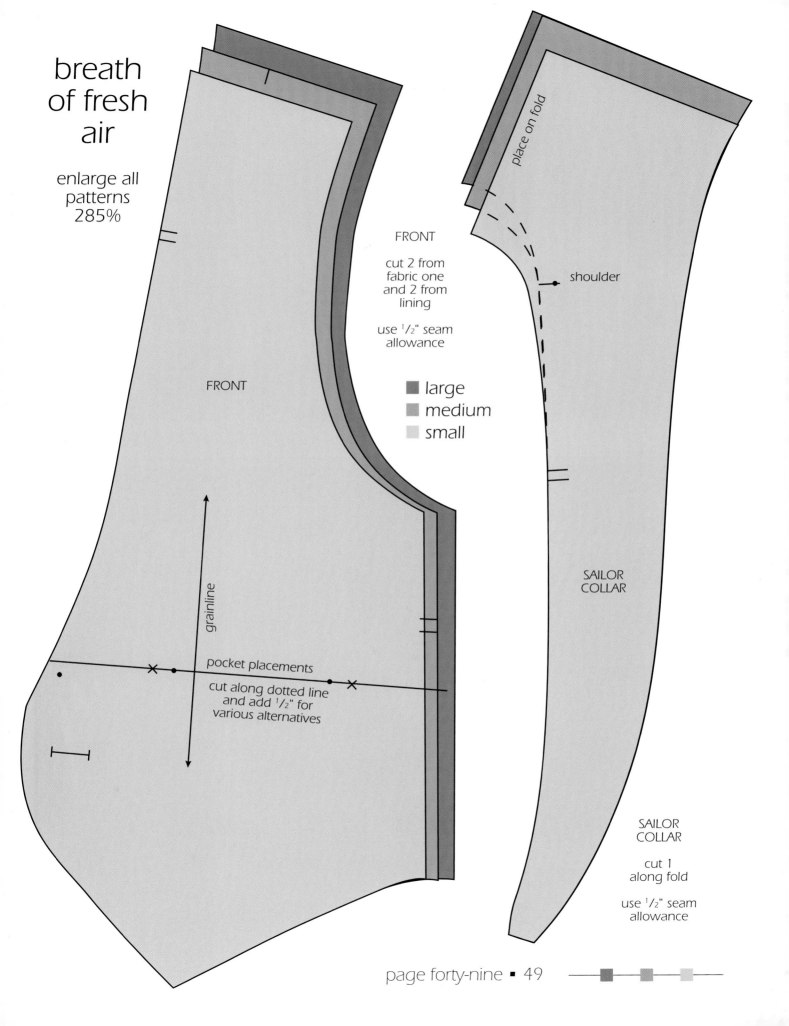

breath
of fresh
air

enlarge all
patterns
285%

FRONT

cut 2 from
fabric one
and 2 from
lining

use 1/2" seam
allowance

■ large
■ medium
■ small

FRONT

grainline

pocket placements

cut along dotted line
and add 1/2" for
various alternatives

place on fold

shoulder

SAILOR
COLLAR

SAILOR
COLLAR

cut 1
along fold

use 1/2" seam
allowance

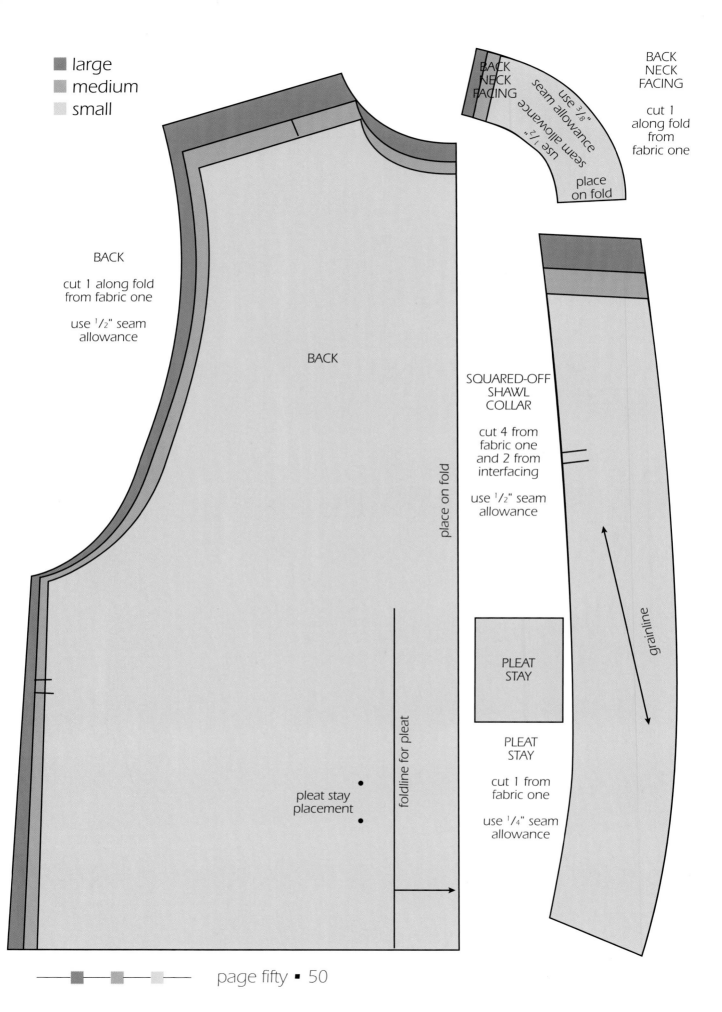

large
medium
small

BACK

cut 1 along fold
from fabric one

use 1/2" seam
allowance

BACK

place on fold

pleat stay
placement

foldline for pleat

BACK
NECK
FACING

use 3/8"
seam allowance

use 1/2"
seam allowance

place
on fold

BACK
NECK
FACING

cut 1
along fold
from
fabric one

SQUARED-OFF
SHAWL
COLLAR

cut 4 from
fabric one
and 2 from
interfacing

use 1/2" seam
allowance

grainline

PLEAT
STAY

PLEAT
STAY

cut 1 from
fabric one

use 1/4" seam
allowance

young at heart

You are a woman content with who you are. Sweet, innocent, playful, and young at heart. Fill your wardrobe with the whimsy that you adore when you create this casual vest.

young at heart . . .
the basic vest

young
at heart

materials needed

fabric one:
 44"- to 60"-wide,
 1 yard
lining:
 44"-wide,
 $^7/_8$ yard or
 54"- to 60"-wide,
 $^3/_4$ yard
fusible interfacing:
 18"-wide,
 $^2/_3$ yard
buttons:
 decorative,
 various
 sizes (5)

IMPORTANT:

- Before beginning, it is recommended that you carefully read "learning the basics" on pages 5-21 and "collars & pockets" on pages 22-33.
- Yardages have been calculated for making the basic vest in a medium size. Adjust yardage amounts accordingly for collars, pockets, and variations in size or fabric usage.

1. cutting fabrics

fabric one:
 front, cut 2
 back, cut 2
 back yoke,
 cut 2
lining:
 front, cut 2
 back, cut 2
fusible interfacing:
 front interfacing,
 cut 2
 cut 1"-wide
 bias strips, 36"

- Do not seam fusible interfacing bias pieces.

- Transfer all markings from pattern to vest pieces.

- Stitch vest in an assembly line manner for speedier results.

2. preparing vest pieces

Trim front edge of interfacing piece so there is a $^1/_8$" seam allowance on all edges except the inward edge. Fuse interfacing to front edge. Fuse bias interfacing strips to remaining bottom edges of front and to bottom edges of back, placing interfacing $^3/_8$" in from cut edges and seam edges.

When adding a collar, trim collar interfacing pieces so there is a $^1/_8$" seam allowance on all edges. Fuse interfacing to the wrong sides of collar pieces.

Prepare collar at this time according to instructions on pages 23-28.

When adding pockets, fuse the interfacing to the wrong side of the pocket pieces.

Prepare pockets at this time according to instructions on pages 29-32.

3. stitching beginning vest elements

When adding a hood, stitch the notched edge of the hood, taking a $^1/_2$" seam. Fold the straight edge of the hood down along the foldline. Turn raw edge under $^1/_4$" and stitch hem in place. Fold and pleat the hood at neck edge where indicated and baste-stitch in place.

Stitch dart in fabric back, and lining back. Press darts toward center back.

young at heart . . .
the basic vest

Stitch fabric center back seam and lining center back seam to dot. Press center back seams open.

Stitch fabric back yoke to top edge of back, matching center back and notches. Press seam toward yoke. Topstitch back yoke $1/4$" from the seam.

Stitch remaining fabric back yoke to top edge of lining back in the same manner. Press yoke seam open.

Follow instructions on pages 17-18 and pages 29-32 to add patch pockets and/or pocket flaps to vest fronts.

Stitch fronts to back at shoulder seams and stitch lining at shoulder seams. Press fabric at shoulder seams toward back yoke. Topstitch $1/4$" from seams. Press lining seams open.

When adding a shirt collar, mandarin collar, or hood, pin assembled collar/hood to front and back neck edges, matching notches and shoulder marks. Baste-stitch shirt collar underside to right side of neck. Baste-stitch mandarin collar or hood to neck, right sides together.

4. stitching lining to vest

Pin lining to vest, right sides together, matching front edge notch, shoulder and center back neck seams and armhole edges.

Stitch back neck, vest front edges, and armhole edges taking a $1/2$" seam.

Cut bulk from corners, grade seam allowances, and clip curves.

Edge-press all seams. Turn right side out, pulling the front through the shoulders toward the back.

5. stitching side seams, vest lower edge

Pin and stitch front to back at side seams, matching notches and armhole seams, taking a $1/2$" seam. In a continuous seam from outer fabric, pin and stitch lining front to back at side seams, matching notches. At one lining side seam, leave a $4 1/2$" opening.

Press side seams open.

Pin and stitch lower edges of vest to vest lining, right sides together, matching seams, taking a $1/2$" seam and breaking stitches at the dot. Do not catch center back seam to itself when stitching to dot.

Cut bulk from corners, grade seam allowances, and clip curves.

Edge-press lower vest seam. Turn right side out through lining side seam opening.

Press thoroughly. Begin by pressing vest edges from lining side and working small sections at a time.

Slipstitch lining side seam opening closed.

When topstitching is desired, measure and mark vest front and back for topstitching placement and stitch through all thicknesses on marks.
For some vest styles, you will find it helpful to topstitch as close to the vest edges as possible.

Topstitching $1/4$" from all edges is also an attractive finish.

Topstitch armhole edges $1/4$" from seam.

6. finishing

Press vest again thoroughly, using a moistened press cloth, if necessary.

Mark and stitch five buttonholes on right front. Stitch five buttons in place on left front.

If desired, on right front, make a 1" long chain-stitched thread loop at right front top edge. On left front, stitch a button where indicated on pattern.

the basic vest . . .

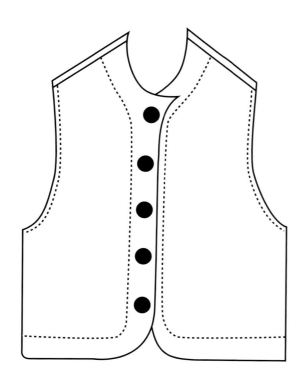

This is a playful vest with simple lines that allow the fabrics chosen to be the center of attention. The dropped shoulder line and back yoke add interest. Five regular buttonholes and buttons are used, but any number of buttons can be used as an alternative that adds simplicity or drama. The same fabric for the vest was used for the lining.

If desired, armhole binding can be added.

The sample vest was made from the following materials:
Fabric one: felt, royal blue
Lining: felt, royal blue
Decorative buttons: porcelain

Actual vest shown on pages 52 & 54

adding a
shirt collar &
patch pockets

. . . adding a shirt collar & patch pockets

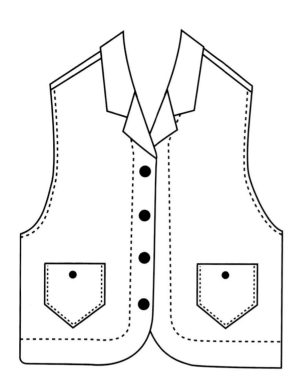

The playful vest is transformed by adding a collar — in this case, a shirt collar. In addition, an ordinary patch pocket has been added on each side. To allow space for the collar, only four regular buttonholes and buttons are used, and buttons have been added to the patch pockets. If desired, topstitching can be added to accentuate the simple lines and a variation to the number of buttonholes and buttons can be made.

The sample vest was made from the following materials:
Fabric one: textured fabric, black/ecru
Lining: textured fabric, black/ecru
Collar: linen weave, black
Pocket lining: cotton broadcloth, black
Decorative buttons: black/gold, $7/8"$ (4); $5/8"$ (2)

Actual vest shown on page 57

. . . adding a
shirt collar &
pleated patch
pockets with
pocket flaps

. . . adding a shirt collar & pleated patch pockets with pocket flaps

Artist's rendition of vest
shown on page 59

A shirt collar, added to the basic vest, completes the look for the outdoors lover. The shirt collar, combined with the dropped shoulders, gives this vest a true look for nature. In addition, a pleated patch pocket has been added on each side and are placed as top pockets. In this instance, no buttons are used. Depending on the style of fabric used for this vest, it can be made into a "safari"-type vest. This particular style of pleated patch pocket with a pocket flap is sometimes referred to as a safari pocket. If desired, topstitching can be added around the vest and around each pocket.

. . . adding a hood & patch pockets

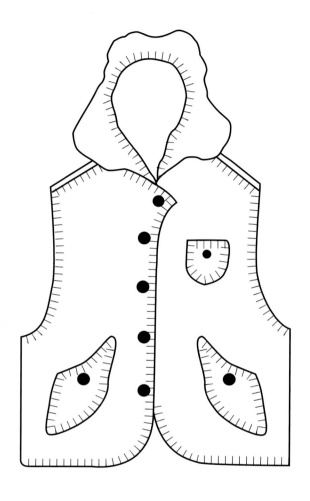

Artist's rendition of vest
shown on page 61

Adding a hood to any vest will give the vest an added functional element — the hood can be used as a hood or worn down the back in a casual manner. In addition, an ordinary patch pocket has been added on each side and a small patch pocket has been added as a top pocket. Five regular buttonholes and buttons are used and buttons have been added to the patch pockets. A slightly smaller button has been used on the top pocket. To accentuate the vest, blanket-stitching has been added around all outside edges, including the hood and pocket edges.

. . . adding a
hood &
patch pockets

... adding a
mandarin collar
& patch pockets

... adding a mandarin collar & patch pockets

young at heart

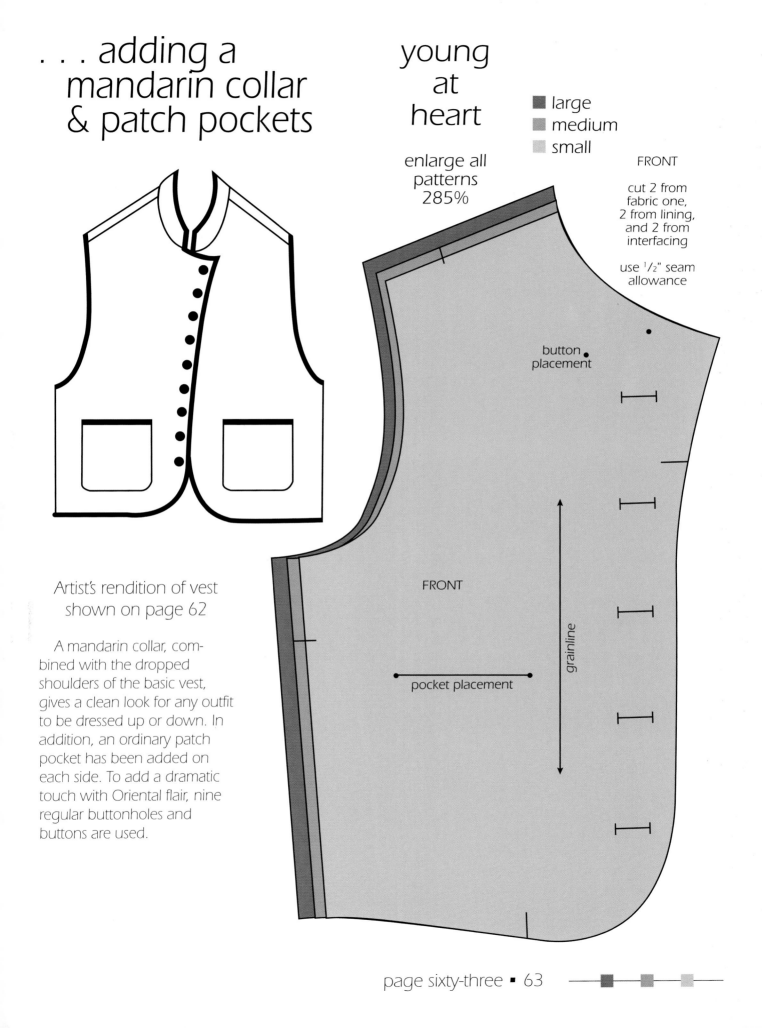

enlarge all patterns 285%

■ large
■ medium
■ small

FRONT

cut 2 from fabric one, 2 from lining, and 2 from interfacing

use ¹/₂" seam allowance

button placement

FRONT

grainline

pocket placement

Artist's rendition of vest shown on page 62

A mandarin collar, combined with the dropped shoulders of the basic vest, gives a clean look for any outfit to be dressed up or down. In addition, an ordinary patch pocket has been added on each side. To add a dramatic touch with Oriental flair, nine regular buttonholes and buttons are used.

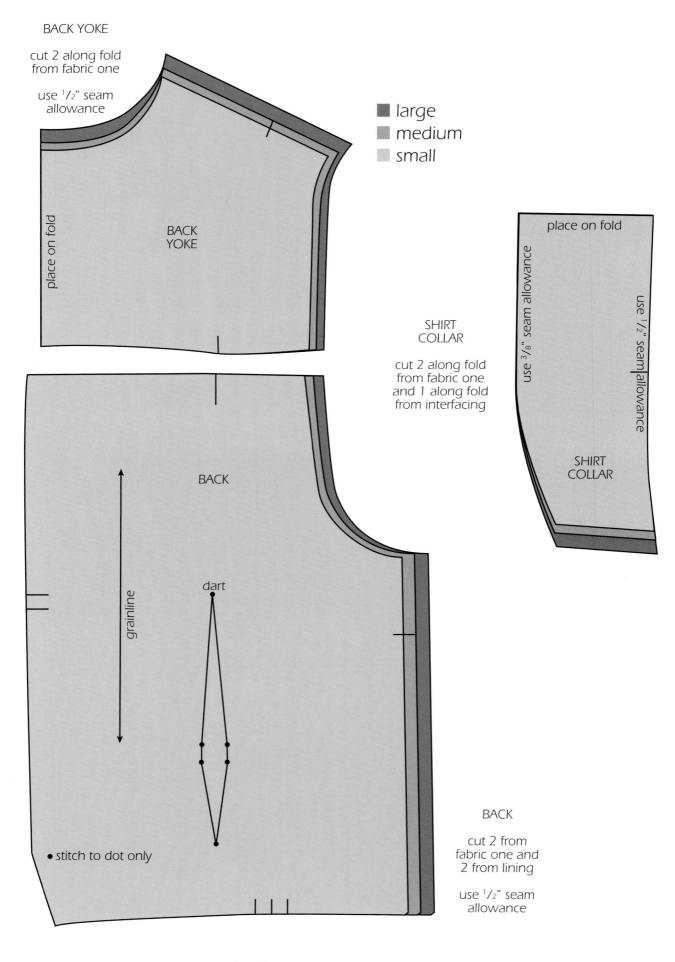

BACK YOKE

cut 2 along fold
from fabric one

use ¹/₂" seam
allowance

place on fold

BACK
YOKE

large
medium
small

place on fold

use ³/₈" seam allowance

use ¹/₂" seam allowance

SHIRT
COLLAR

cut 2 along fold
from fabric one
and 1 along fold
from interfacing

SHIRT
COLLAR

grainline

dart

BACK

• stitch to dot only

BACK

cut 2 from
fabric one and
2 from lining

use ¹/₂" seam
allowance

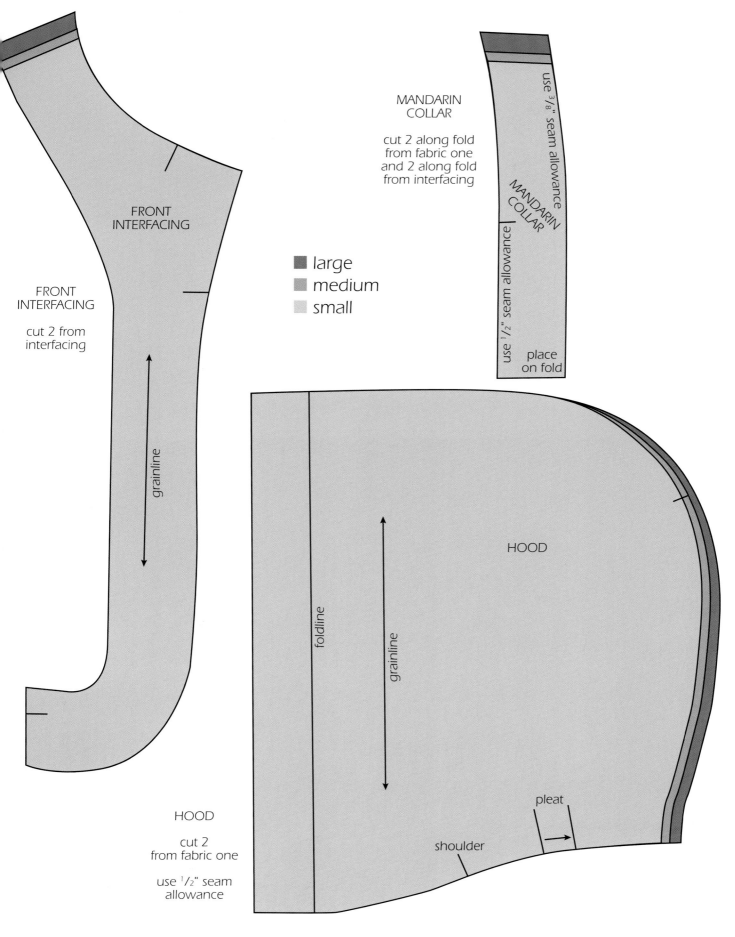

FRONT
INTERFACING

FRONT
INTERFACING

cut 2 from
interfacing

grainline

MANDARIN
COLLAR

cut 2 along fold
from fabric one
and 2 along fold
from interfacing

■ large
■ medium
■ small

use ⅜" seam allowance

MANDARIN
COLLAR

use ½" seam allowance

place
on fold

HOOD

foldline

grainline

HOOD

cut 2
from fabric one

use ½" seam
allowance

shoulder

pleat

the gentle
side . . .
the
basic
vest

Suddenly, 9 to 5,
meetings, and messages
lose their meaning.
In the office you are
efficient, ambitious, and strong.
But at home,
another side of you is revealed.
A gentle side —
soft, feminine, and romantic.
This double-breasted vest
can help capture
your gentle side.

the gentle side

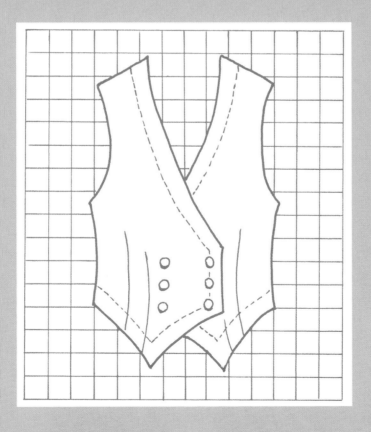

the gentle
side . . .
the
basic
vest

the gentle side

materials needed

fabric one:
   44"-wide,
   $7/8$ yard or
   54"- to 60"-wide,
   $3/4$ yard
fabric two:
   44"- to 60"-wide,
   $2/3$ yard
lining:
   44"-wide,
   $1 1/4$ yards or
   54"- to 60"-wide,
   1 yard
fusible interfacing:
   18"-wide,
   $7/8$ yard
buttons:
   decorative,
   various
   sizes (6)
   clear, $1/2$" (1)

IMPORTANT:
▪ Before beginning, it is recommended that you carefully read "learning the basics" on pages 5-21 and "collars & pockets" on pages 22-33.

▪ Yardages have been calculated for making the basic vest in a medium size. Adjust yardage amounts accordingly for collars, pockets, and variations in size or fabric usage.

1. cutting fabrics

fabric one:
   front, cut 2
   side, cut 2
fabric two:
   back, cut 2
   armhole binding,
      cut 2"-wide
      bias strips, 48"
lining:
   front, cut 2
   side, cut 2
   back, cut 2
fusible interfacing:
   front edge,
      cut 2
      (see pattern
      for cutting line)
      cut 1"-wide
      bias strips, 42"

▪ For armhole binding, cut enough bias strips for a total of 48" in length and seam together. When adding a collar to the basic vest, additional bias may be needed.

▪ Do not seam fusible interfacing bias pieces.

▪ Transfer all markings from pattern to vest pieces.

▪ Stitch vest in an assembly line manner for speedier results.

2. preparing vest pieces

Trim front edge of interfacing piece so there is a $1/8$" seam allowance on all edges except the "cut interfacing to here" line. Fuse interfacing to front edge. Fuse bias interfacing strips to bottom edges of front, back, and sides, placing interfacing $3/8$" in from cut edges and seam edges. Do not fuse interfacing over dart stitch lines.

When adding a collar, trim collar interfacing pieces so there is a $1/8$" seam allowance on all edges. Fuse interfacing to the wrong sides of collar pieces.

Prepare collar at this time according to instructions on pages 23-28.

3. stitching beginning vest elements

Stitch fabric center back seam and lining center back seam to dot.

Stitch fabric front darts and lining front darts.

Press center back seams open. Press front darts toward front edge.

When adding a collar, pin assembled collar to front neck edge and shoulders matching notches. Baste-stitch, having collar underside against right side of front.

Stitch sides to fronts and lining sides to fronts.

Press seams toward sides. Press lining seams open.

Stitch fronts to backs at shoulder seams and stitch lining at shoulder seams.

Press seams toward front. Press lining seams open.

Topstitch $1/4$" from shoulder and side seams and press.

4. stitching lining to vest

Pin lining to vest, right sides together, matching front edge notch, shoul-

der, and center back neck seams.

Stitch back neck and vest front edges, taking a $1/2$" seam.

Cut bulk from corners, grade seam allowances, and clip curves.

Edge-press all seams. Turn right side out.

5. stitching side seams, vest lower edge

Pin and stitch side to back at side seams, matching notches and armhole seams, taking a $1/2$" seam allowance. In a continuous seam from outer fabric, pin and stitch lining side to back at side seams, matching notches. At one lining side seam, leave a $41/2$" opening.

Press side seams open.

Pin and stitch lower edges of vest to vest lining, right sides together,

matching seams and darts, taking a $1/2$" seam allowance and breaking stitches at the dot. At center back bottom seam edge, make certain to match lining to fabric at dots. Do not catch center back seam to itself when stitching to dot.

Cut bulk from corners, grade seam allowances, and clip curves.

Edge-press lower vest edge seam. Turn right side out through lining side seam opening.

Press thoroughly. Begin by pressing vest edges from lining side and working small sections at a time.

Slipstitch lining side seam opening closed.

When topstitching is desired, measure and mark vest front or back for topstitching placement and stitch through all thicknesses on marks. For some vest

styles, you will find it helpful to top-stitch as close to vest edges as possible, including underneath a collar when applicable.

Topstitching $1/4$" from all edges is also an attractive finish.

6. binding armholes with bias

Pin lining to vest at armholes. Beginning at the side seam, stitch bias to armhole, taking a $1/2$" seam. Leave a $1/2$" seam allowance on bias at side seam and begin stitches $3/4$" away from side seam. End stitching $3/4$" prior to side seam.

Align bias ends to side seam and mark. Stitch bias ends together on mark. Trim seam to $3/8$" and press open. Finish stitching bias to armhole at side seam. Trim seam to $1/4$". Press seam toward binding. Turn under remaining edge of bias while folding bias over seam to encase. Pin, so the turned under edge is placed just beyond the seam and so heads of pins face the outward folded edge of bias. Stitch, following stitch-in-the-ditch method.

the basic vest . . .

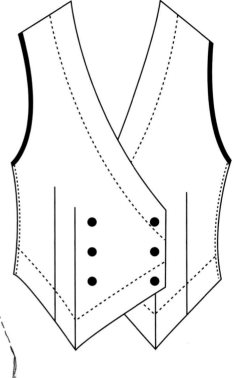

7. finishing

Press vest again thoroughly, using a moistened press cloth, if necessary.

Mark and stitch three buttonholes on right front. Stitch three buttons in place on left front and three buttons in place on right front.

On left front, make a $3/4$" long chainstitched thread loop where indicated on pattern. On inside right front, stitch $1/2$" clear button where indicated on pattern.

The sample vest was made from the following materials:
Fabric one: cotton osnaberg, oatmeal
Fabric two: cotton print, mauve/tan
Lining: sateen stripe, beige on beige
Decorative buttons: faux wood, $11/16$"

This is a dressy double-breasted vest with binding around the armholes and topstitching to accentuate the front and back. The topstitching is done 1" from the vest front and back edges. Darts are made in the front. Three regular buttonholes are used for three of the buttons and the remaining three buttons are placed directly on the right vest front. The fabric used for the back of the vest is also used for the armhole binding.

For armhole binding, cut enough bias strips for a total of 48" in length and seam together. When adding a collar to the basic vest, additional bias may be needed.

Actual vest shown on pages 66 & 68

. . . adding a
shawl collar

. . . adding a shawl collar

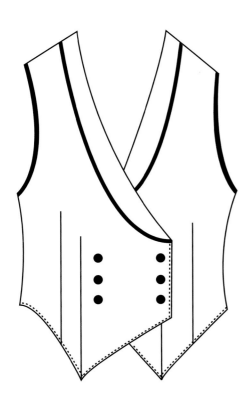

Adding a shawl collar with bias binding re-designs the basic double-breasted vest. In addition to binding around the armholes, binding is also added around the collar and the topstitching is close to the edges. The collar ends at the shoulders and darts are made in the front. Three regular buttonholes are used for three of the buttons and the remaining three buttons are placed directly on the right vest front. The fabric used for the lining of the vest is also used for the armhole and collar binding.

For armhole and collar binding, cut enough bias strips for a total of 88" in length and seam together.

The sample vest was made from the following materials:
    Fabric one: jacquard, gray with ecru
    Fabric two: velveteen, olive green
    Lining: cotton tweed, gray
    Decorative buttons: pewter, $3/4$"

Actual vest shown on page 72

. . . adding a
notch collar

. . . adding a notch collar

Artist's rendition of vest
shown on page 74

A notch collar transforms this double-breasted vest into a true fashion statement. Binding is repeated around the armholes, and the topstitching is close to the edges. The collar ends at the shoulders and darts are made in the front. Three regular buttonholes are used for three of the buttons and the remaining three buttons are placed directly on the right vest front. The fabric used for the back or the lining of the vest can be used for the armhole binding.

When using bias around armholes and around collars, cut enough bias strips for the total length and seam together.

. . . adding a squared-off shawl collar

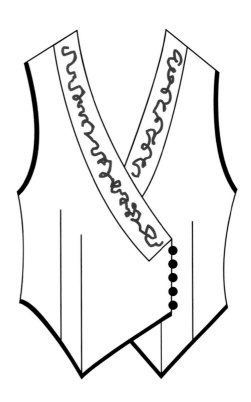

Artist's rendition of vest
shown on page 76

Add a splash of sophistication to the basic vest with the addition of a squared-off shawl collar. The ribbon trim adds a special touch of femininity. Binding is repeated around the armholes and the vest bottom edges, but the topstitching is eliminated. The collar ends at the shoulders. Darts are made in the front and five or six looped buttonholes and buttons are used. The fabric used for the back or the lining of the vest can be used for the armhole binding.

When using bias around the armholes and around the collars, cut enough bias strips for the total length and seam together.

. . . adding a
squared-off
shawl collar

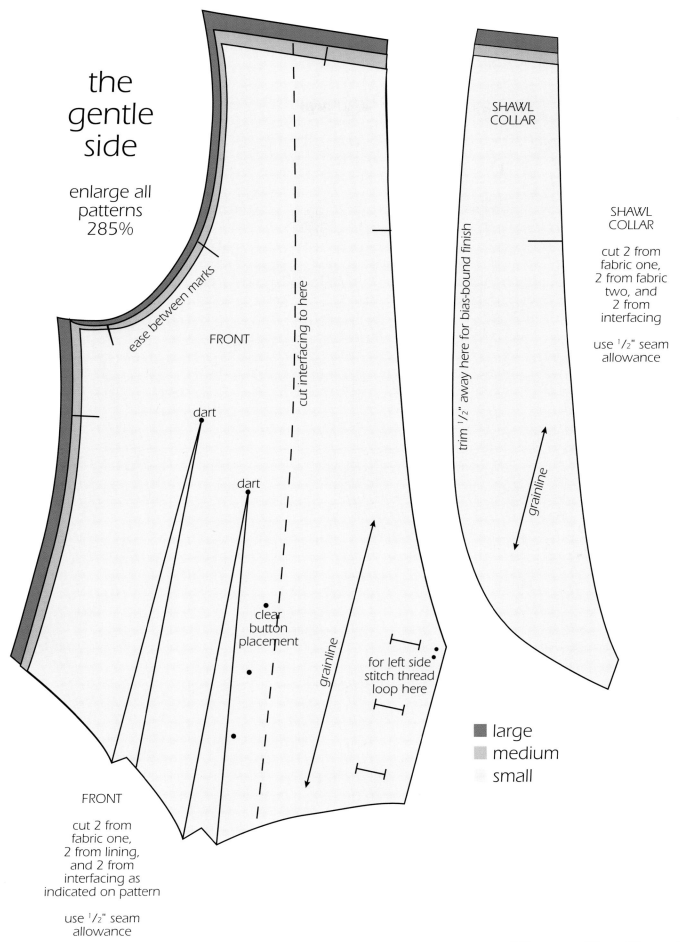

the gentle side

enlarge all patterns 285%

ease between marks

FRONT

cut interfacing to here

dart

dart

clear button placement

grainline

grainline

for left side stitch thread loop here

SHAWL COLLAR

SHAWL COLLAR

cut 2 from fabric one, 2 from fabric two, and 2 from interfacing

use ¹/₂" seam allowance

trim ¹/₂" away here for bias-bound finish

grainline

FRONT

cut 2 from fabric one, 2 from lining, and 2 from interfacing as indicated on pattern

use ¹/₂" seam allowance

■ large
■ medium
□ small

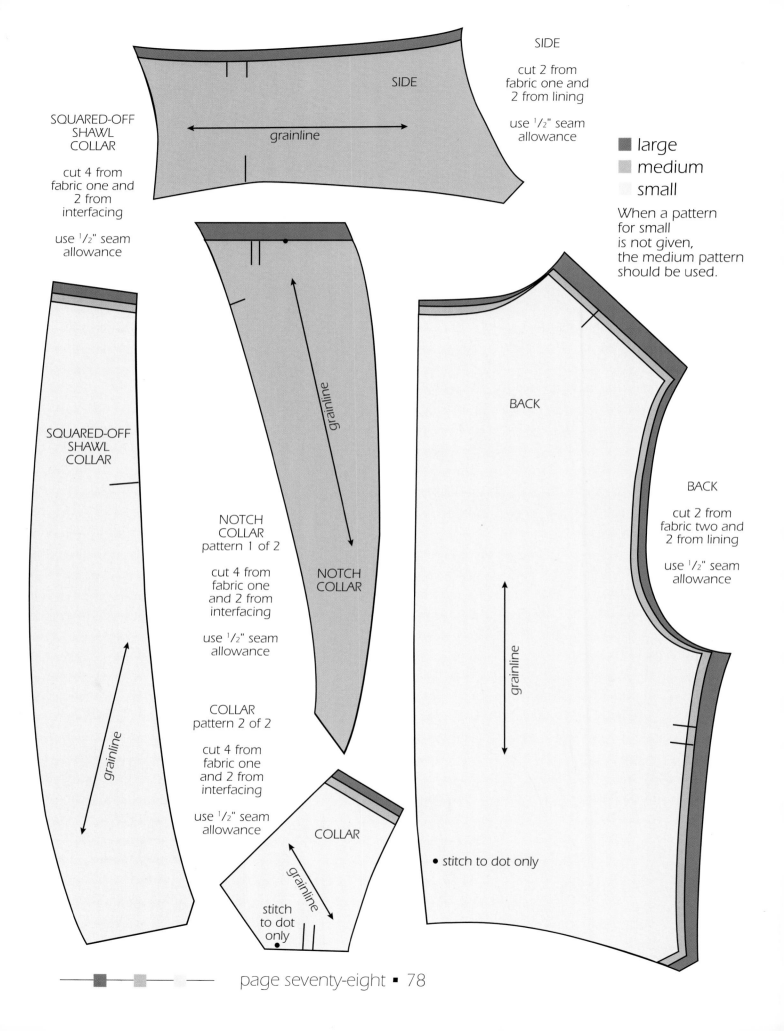

SIDE

SQUARED-OFF
SHAWL
COLLAR

cut 4 from
fabric one and
2 from
interfacing

use ¹/₂" seam
allowance

grainline

SIDE

cut 2 from
fabric one and
2 from lining

use ¹/₂" seam
allowance

■ large
■ medium
□ small

When a pattern
for small
is not given,
the medium pattern
should be used.

SQUARED-OFF
SHAWL
COLLAR

BACK

grainline

NOTCH
COLLAR
pattern 1 of 2

cut 4 from
fabric one
and 2 from
interfacing

use ¹/₂" seam
allowance

NOTCH
COLLAR

BACK

cut 2 from
fabric two and
2 from lining

use ¹/₂" seam
allowance

COLLAR
pattern 2 of 2

cut 4 from
fabric one
and 2 from
interfacing

use ¹/₂" seam
allowance

grainline

grainline

COLLAR

grainline

stitch
to dot
only

• stitch to dot only

Memories are
precious to you.
Moments of happiness,
days of joy —
each has a place
in your heart.
You will find that place
— now and forever —
while wearing this simply
elegant and versatile vest.
Try any one of the
vests with subtle
changes and begin
creating new memories today.

now and forever

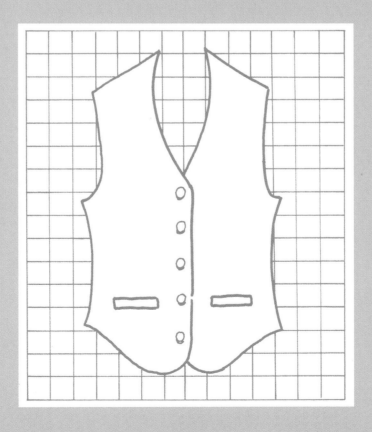

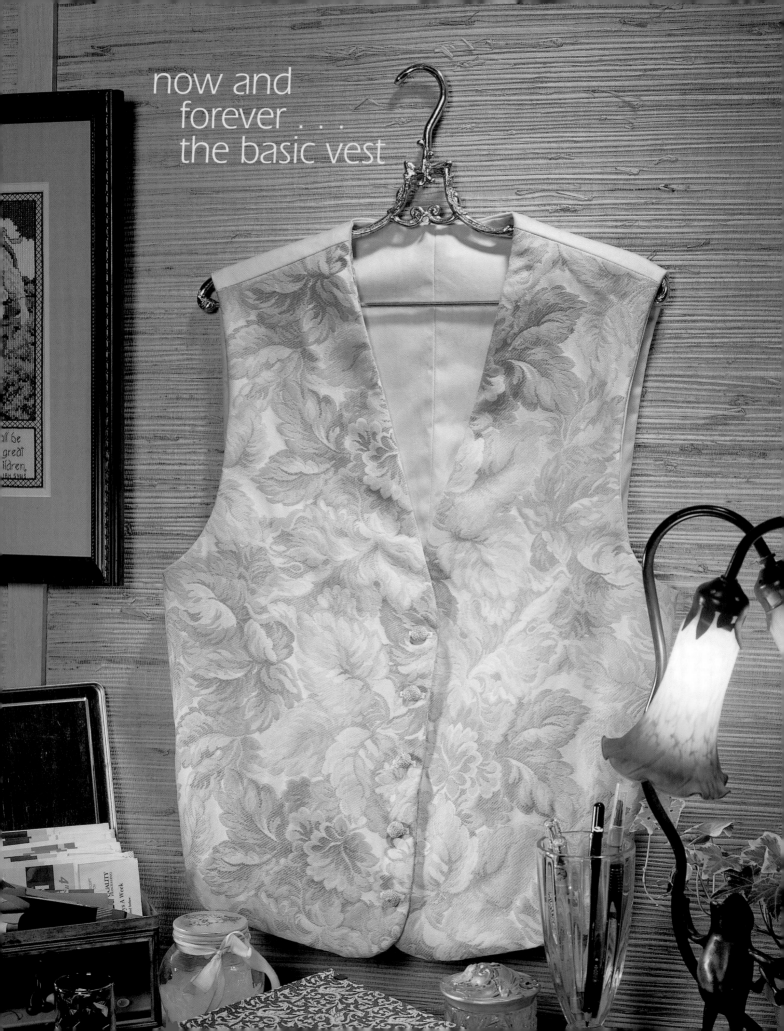

now and
forever . . .
the basic vest

now and forever

materials needed

fabric one:
   44"- to 60"-wide,
   $^7/_8$ yard
fabric two:
   44"- to 60"-wide,
   $^3/_4$ yard
lining:
   44"- to 60"-wide,
   $1^1/_8$ yards
fusible interfacing:
   18"-wide,
   $^7/_8$ yard
buttons:
   decorative,
   various
   sizes (7)

IMPORTANT:
• Before beginning, it is recommended that you carefully read "learning the basics" on pages 5-21 and "collars & pockets" on pages 22-33.

• Yardages have been calculated for making the basic vest in a medium size. Adjust yardage amounts accordingly for collars, pockets, and variations in size or fabric usage.

1. cutting fabrics

fabric one:
   front, cut 2
   back belt, cut 4
fabric two:
   back, cut 2
lining:
   front, cut 2
   back, cut 2
fusible interfacing:
   front edge,
   cut 2
   (see pattern
   for cutting line)
   cut 1"-wide
   bias strips, 36"
   back belt, cut 2

• Do not seam fusible interfacing bias pieces.

• Transfer all markings from pattern to vest pieces.

• Stitch vest in an assembly line manner for speedier results.

2. preparing vest pieces

Trim front edge of interfacing piece so there is a $^1/_8$" seam allowance on all edges except the "cut interfacing to here" line. Trim back belt interfacing pieces so there is a $^1/_8$" seam allowance on all edges. Fuse interfacing to front edge. Fuse bias interfacing strips to remaining bottom edges of front and to bottom edges of back, placing interfacing $^3/_8$" in from cut edges and seam edges. Fuse interfacing to two back belts.

When adding a collar, trim collar interfacing pieces so there is a $^1/_8$" seam allowance on all edges. Fuse interfacing to the wrong sides of collar pieces.

Prepare collar at this time according to instructions on pages 23-28.

When adding pockets, fuse the interfacing to the wrong side of the pocket pieces.

Prepare pockets at this time according to instructions on pages 29-32.

3. stitching beginning vest elements

Stitch back darts and lining back darts. Clip darts and press toward center back.

Stitch back fabric center back seam and lining center back seam to dot. Press center back seams open.

now and
forever . . .
the basic vest

When adding fake welt pockets, fold pocket in half, right sides together, matching notched edges. Stitch short ends, taking a $3/8$" seam allowance. Trim bulk and edge-press seams. Turn right side out and press. Pin welt to each front, right sides together, having raw edges of welt $1/2$" above indicated line. Stitch $1/2$" from edge. Trim seam allowance to $1/4$". Press welt upward covering raw edges. Machine- or hand-stitch ends of welt to front.

Follow instructions on pages 17-18 and pages 29-32 to add patch pockets and/or pocket flaps to vest fronts.

When adding a soft-notch or rounded shawl collar, pin assembled collar to front neck edge and shoulders matching notches. Baste-stitch, having collar underside against

right side of front.

Pin and stitch interfaced back belts to remaining back belts, right sides together, taking a $3/8$" seam allowance. Do not stitch short, straight edge. Trim bulk from corners, grade seam allowances, and edge-press seams. Turn right side out and press.

Pin and baste-stitch unstitched edge of back belt to back side seam where indicated on pattern. Measure inward from side seam $2 1/2$" on back belt. Topstitch back belt to back along edges and up to mark.

Stitch fronts to back at shoulder seams and stitch lining at shoulder seams.

Press shoulder seams open.

When adding a notch or kimono collar, pin assembled collar to front and back neck edges, matching notches and shoul-

der marks. Baste-stitch, having collar underside against right side of front and back.

4. stitching lining to vest

Pin lining to vest, right sides together, matching front edge notch, shoulder and center back neck seams and armhole edges.

Stitch back neck, vest front edges, and armhole edges, taking a $1/2$" seam.

Cut bulk from corners, grade seam allowances, and clip curves.

Edge-press all seams. Turn right side out, pulling the front through the shoulders toward the back.

5. stitching side seams, vest lower edge

Pin and stitch front to back at side seams, matching

notches and armhole seams, taking a $1/2$" seam. In a continuous seam from outer fabric, pin and stitch lining front to back at side seams, matching notches. At one lining side seam, leave a $4 1/2$" opening.

Press side seams open.

Pin and stitch lower edges of vest to vest lining, right sides together, matching seams, taking a $1/2$" seam and breaking stitches at the dot. Do not catch center back seam to itself when stitching to dot.

Cut bulk from corners, grade seam allowances, and clip curves.

Edge-press lower vest seam. Turn right side out through lining side seam opening.

Press thoroughly. Begin by pressing vest edges from lining side and working small sections at a time.

Slipstitch lining side seam opening closed.

When topstitching is desired, topstitch vest front as close to edges as possible, including stitching underneath a collar when applicable. Topstitching $1/4$" from all edges is also an attractive finish.

6. finishing

Press vest again thoroughly, using a moistened press cloth, if necessary.

Mark and stitch five buttonholes on right front and two buttonholes on right back belt. Stitch five buttons in place on left front and two buttons in place on left back belt.

the basic vest . . .

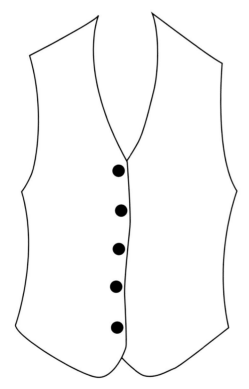

The sample vest was made from the following materials:
   Fabric one: tapestry, floral
   Fabric two: polished cotton, gold
   Lining: polished cotton, gold
   Decorative buttons: gold-cord wrapped

Actual vest shown on pages 80 & 82

This is a simple vest that offers the versatility from down-to-earth to elegance with its soft, curved lines and v-neck. The basic vest offers five regular buttonholes and buttons in the front and two on the back belt.

. . . adding a
soft-notch collar
& patch pockets
with pocket flaps

. . . adding a soft-notch collar & patch pockets with pocket flaps

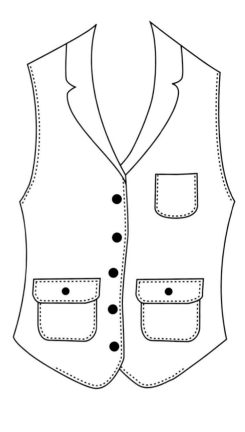

A soft-notch collar has been added to this vest for a touch of femininity. In addition, an ordinary patch pocket with pocket flaps has been added on each side and a smaller patch pocket without a pocket flap has been added as a top pocket. The collar ends at the shoulders. Five regular buttonholes and buttons are used, and buttons have been added to the patch pockets that have pocket flaps.

The sample vest was made from the following materials:
Fabric one: cotton print fabric, periwinkle/multi
Fabric two: cotton knit fabric, pale yellow
Lining: cotton stripe fabric, yellow/white
Decorative buttons: fabric covered, yellow (9)

Actual vest shown on page 85

...adding a
notch collar &
pleated patch
pockets with
pocket flaps

. . . adding a notch collar & pleated patch pockets with pocket flaps

Adding a notch collar and pleated patch pockets with pocket flaps to this vest changes the look from basic to casual. Five regular buttonholes and buttons are used, and buttons have been added to the patch pockets. Top-stitching is added to create dimension and give warmth to the overall look of the vest.

The sample vest was made from the following materials:
Fabric one: cotton plaid fabric, blue/tan
Fabric two: wool, tan
Lining: cotton print fabric, blue/multi
Decorative buttons: brass (9)

Actual vest shown on page 87

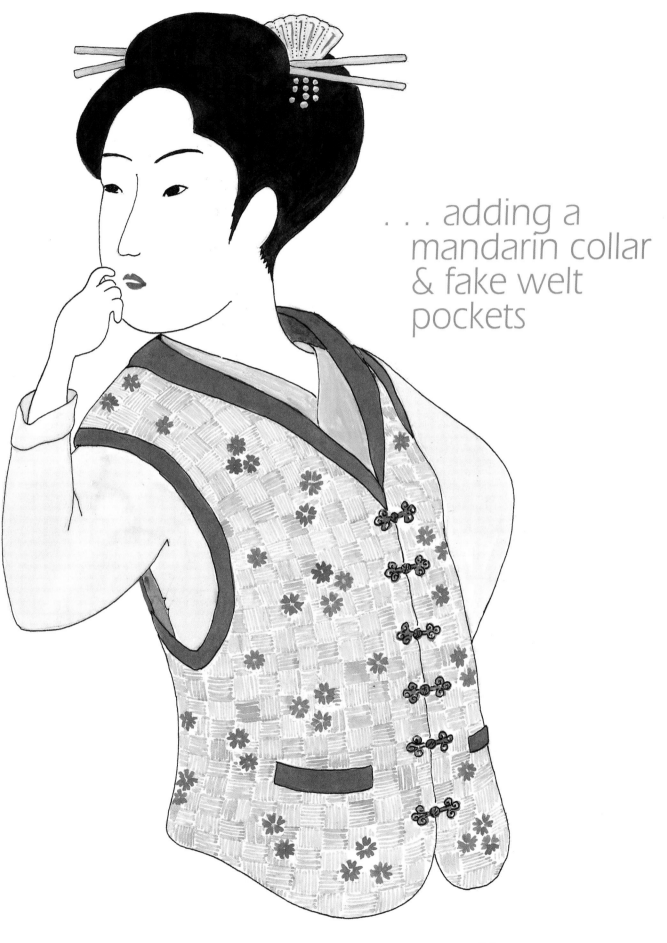

. . . adding a
mandarin collar
& fake welt
pockets

. . . adding a mandarin collar & fake welt pockets

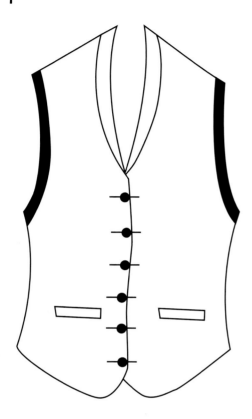

Artist's rendition of vest
shown on page 89

The shape of the mandarin collar sets the mood for this vest and the feel is enhanced by adding frogs around the buttons. One additional button is added and the combination of the collar and the buttons add height. In addition, a fake welt pocket has been added to each side and extra-wide bias was used for binding around the armholes.

When using bias around armholes and collars, cut enough bias strips for the total length and seam together.

. . . adding a rounded collar & rounded patch pockets

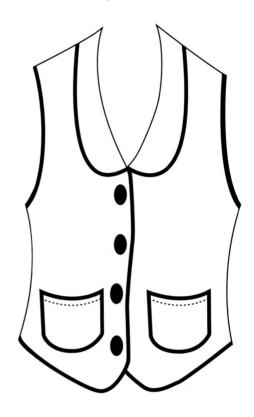

Artist's rendition of vest
shown on page 91

Here, a rounded collar has been added to give this vest a free-flowing, comfortable look with the collar ending at the shoulders. Only four regular buttonholes and buttons adorn the front of this vest which also adds to its uncluttered look. Rounded patch pockets are added at each side. Using a soft-knit fabric will make this vest look unrestricted.

. . . adding a
rounded collar
& rounded
patch pockets

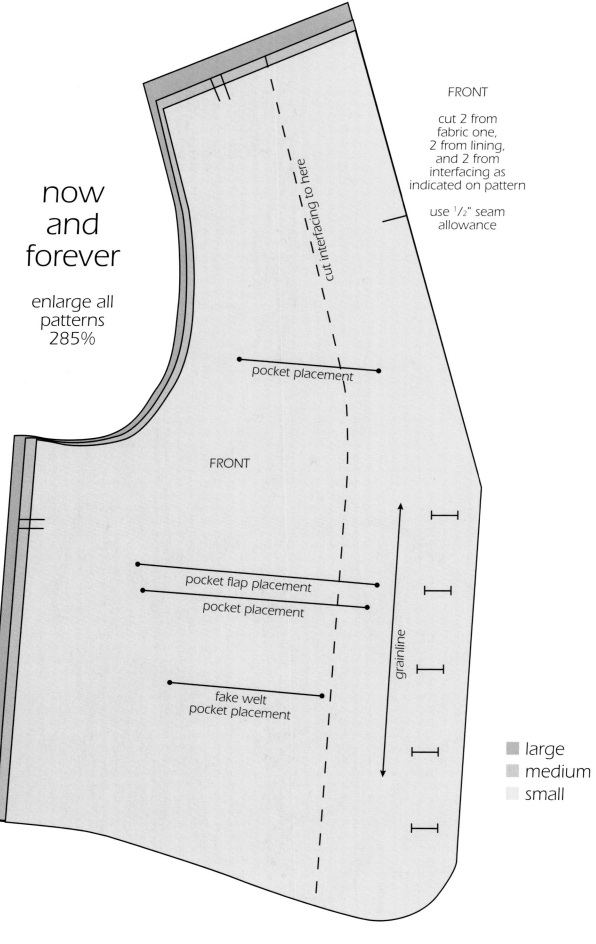

now
and
forever

enlarge all
patterns
285%

FRONT

cut 2 from
fabric one,
2 from lining,
and 2 from
interfacing as
indicated on pattern

use $\frac{1}{2}$" seam
allowance

cut interfacing to here

pocket placement

FRONT

pocket flap placement

pocket placement

grainline

fake welt
pocket placement

large
medium
small

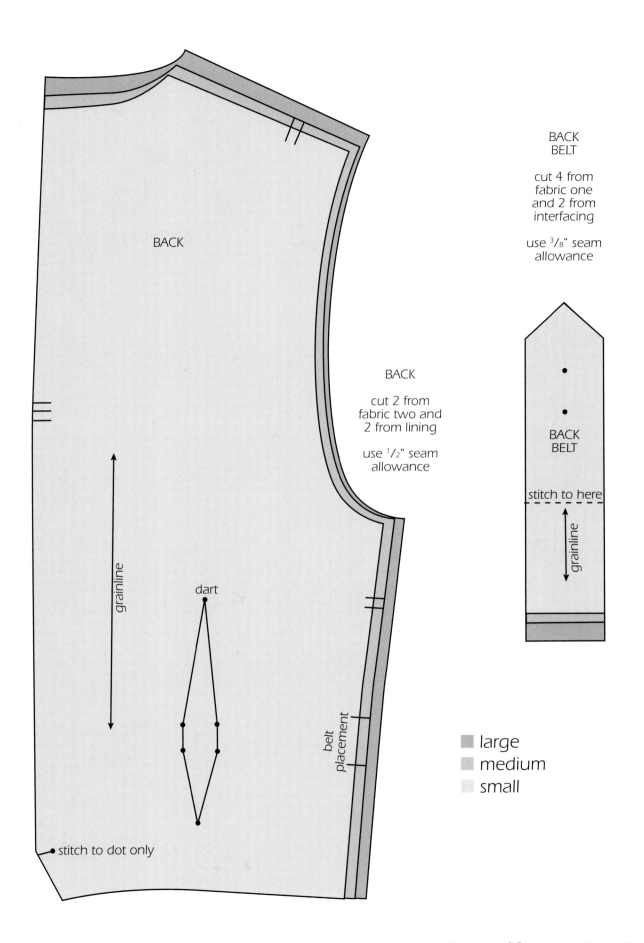

BACK

BACK

cut 2 from
fabric two and
2 from lining

use $1/2$" seam
allowance

grainline

dart

belt
placement

stitch to dot only

BACK
BELT

cut 4 from
fabric one
and 2 from
interfacing

use $3/8$" seam
allowance

BACK
BELT

stitch to here

grainline

⬛ large
⬛ medium
⬜ small

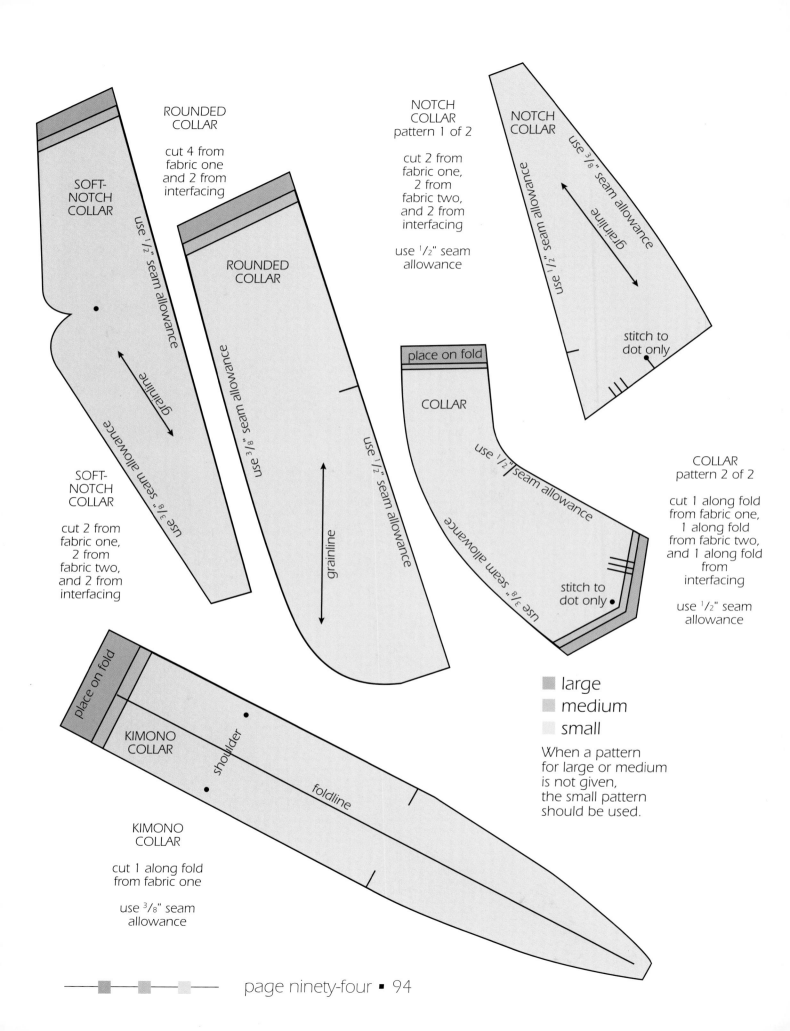

ROUNDED
COLLAR

cut 4 from
fabric one
and 2 from
interfacing

NOTCH
COLLAR
pattern 1 of 2

cut 2 from
fabric one,
2 from
fabric two,
and 2 from
interfacing

use 1/2" seam
allowance

NOTCH
COLLAR

use 3/8" seam allowance

grainline

use 1/2" seam allowance

SOFT-
NOTCH
COLLAR

use 1/2" seam allowance

grainline

ROUNDED
COLLAR

use 3/8" seam allowance

grainline

use 1/2" seam allowance

SOFT-
NOTCH
COLLAR

cut 2 from
fabric one,
2 from
fabric two,
and 2 from
interfacing

use 3/8" seam allowance

place on fold

COLLAR

use 1/2" seam allowance

use 3/8" seam allowance

stitch to
dot only

stitch to
dot only

COLLAR
pattern 2 of 2

cut 1 along fold
from fabric one,
1 along fold
from fabric two,
and 1 along fold
from
interfacing

use 1/2" seam
allowance

▇ large
▇ medium
▇ small

When a pattern
for large or medium
is not given,
the small pattern
should be used.

place on fold

KIMONO
COLLAR

shoulder

foldline

KIMONO
COLLAR

cut 1 along fold
from fabric one

use 3/8" seam
allowance

A walk in the park,
a chat in the rain —
a moment in time.
These are
the moments
to fondly
look back on.
Each moment seems
more special
when you wear
clothes you love.
This tailored vest and its
alternatives will help you
enjoy every moment.

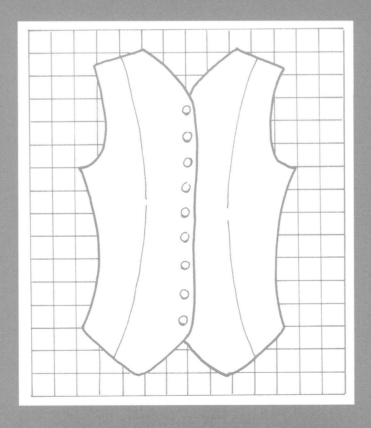

moments in time . . .
the basic vest

moments in time

materials needed

fabric one:
  44"-wide,
  1 1/2 yards
  54"- to 60"-wide,
  1 3/8 yards
fusible interfacing:
  18"-wide,
  1 yard
buttons:
  decorative,
  1/2" (11)

IMPORTANT:
- Before beginning, it is recommended that you carefully read "learning the basics" on pages 5-21 and "collars & pockets" on pages 22-33.
- Yardages have been calculated for making the basic vest in a medium size. Adjust yardage amounts accordingly for collars, pockets, and variations in size or fabric usage.

1. cutting fabrics

fabric one:
  front, cut 4
  side front, cut 2
  side back, cut 2
  back, cut 1
    along fold
  back facing,
    cut 1 along fold
  armhole binding,
    cut 1 7/8"-wide
    bias strips, 40"
fusible interfacing:
  front, cut 2
    (see pattern
    for cutting line)
  back facing,
    cut 1 along fold
  cut 1"-wide
    bias strips, 36"

- For armhole binding, cut enough bias strips for a total of 40" in length and seam together. When adding a collar to the basic vest, additional fabric may be needed.

- Do not seam fusible interfacing bias pieces.

- Transfer all markings from pattern to vest pieces.

- Stitch vest in an assembly line manner for speedier results.

2. preparing vest pieces

Trim front interfacing and back facing interfacing pieces so there is a 1/8" seam allowance on all edges, except the "cut interfacing to here" line.

Fuse interfacing to one left and one right front and to the back facing. Fuse bias interfacing strips to bottom edges of side front, side back, and back, placing interfacing 1" up from cut edges and 3/8" inward from seam edges.

When adding a collar, trim collar interfacing pieces so there is a 1/8" seam allowance on all edges. Fuse interfacing to the wrong sides of collar pieces.

Prepare collar at this time according to instructions on pages 23-28.

When adding pockets, fuse the interfacing to the wrong side of the pocket pieces.

Prepare pockets at this time according to instructions on pages 29-32.

moments in time....
the basic vest

3. stitching vest seams

Stitch front to side front, right sides together, matching notches and dot at side front hem edge. Stitch again $1/4$" from first row of stitching.

Stitch back to side backs, right sides together, matching notches. Stitch again $1/4$" from first row of stitching.

Trim all seams just past the second row of stitching. Zigzag-stitch over edge of seams (or overlock). Press seams flat. Press vest front seams toward front and press vest back seams toward back.

Follow instructions on pages 17-18 and pages 29-32 to add fake welt or patch pockets to vest fronts.

When adding a rounded collar to the scoop neck vest, pin assembled collar to front neck edge and shoul-

ders, matching notches. Baste-stitch, having collar underside against right side of front.

Stitch front to back at shoulders and side seams, right sides together, matching notches. Stitch again $1/4$" from first row of stitching. Trim seams just past second row of stitching. Zigzag-stitch over edge of seams (or overlock). Press seams flat, then toward back.

When adding a shirt or mandarin collar, pin assembled collar to front and back neck edges, matching notches and shoulder marks. Baste-stitch collar to neck edge, right sides together.

4. preparing facing

Stitch remaining fronts to back facing, right sides together, taking a $1/2$" seam allow-

ance. Press seams open.

Stitch $3/8$" along all outward facing edges, except vest hem edge. Clip curves to stitching.

Press facing edge under along stitching. Stitch close to the edge. Stitch again $1/4$" from the first row of stitching.

5. stitching facing to vest

Pin front and back facing to vest, matching center back, shoulder seams, front edge notches, and front hem edges. Stitch, taking a $1/2$" seam allowance, ending stitches at front dot.

Cut bulk from corners, grade seam allowances, and clip curves.

From vest inside, press facing seam allowances toward facings, as close as the iron will allow. Understitch all edges, under-

stitching as close to the front edge bottom point as the sewing machine will allow. It is not necessary to understitch the front hem edge.

Press thoroughly. Begin by pressing vest edges from facing side and working small sections at a time.

Pin facing in place at all edges. Hand-tack the facing to the vest at the shoulders. If necessary, invisibly hand-tack the front facing edges in place as well.

6. binding armholes with bias & hemming vest

Using seamed bias fabric strips and beginning at the side seam, stitch bias to armhole, taking a $1/2$" seam allowance. Leave a $1/2$" seam allowance on bias at the side seam and begin stitches ¾" away from the side seam. End stitching ¾" prior to side seam.

Align bias ends to side seam and mark. Stitch bias ends together on mark. Trim seam to ³⁄₈" and press open. Finish stitching bias to armhole at side seam. Trim seam to ¹⁄₄". Press seam toward binding. Turn under the remaining edge of the bias while folding the bias over armhole seam to enclose. Pin it so the folded under edge is placed just beyond the seam and so the heads of the pins face the armhole opening. Edgestitch the bias from the right side just to the inside of the seam, catching in folded over edge on the underside. Remove the pins while stitching.

Mark the hem 1¹⁄₄" from the remaining bottom vest edges. Stitch ¹⁄₄" from bottom vest edges. Zigzag-

stitch over edge (or overlock). Press flat.

Fold hem up to the underside on marks and press in place. Pin.

Machine- or hand-blindstitch hem in place.

7. finishing

Press vest again thoroughly, using a moistened press cloth, if necessary.

Mark and stitch eleven buttonholes on right front, or the number of buttonholes desired. Stitch buttons in place on left front.

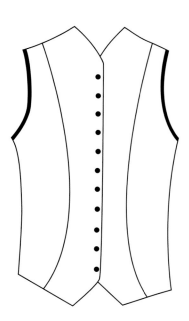

the basic vest . . .

Actual vest shown on pages 96 & 98

This waist-coat style vest gives the illusion of height because of its styling and the princess seams that have been used. Eleven regular buttonholes and buttons are used, but any number of buttons can be used as an alternative that adds simplicity or drama. The bias-bound armholes gives a nice complete finish.

The sample vest was made from the following materials:
Fabric one: brocade, red
Decorative buttons: mother of pearl (11)

adding a
shirt collar &
fake welt
pockets

. . . adding a shirt collar & fake welt pockets

The princess seams on this vest, combined with the shirt collar and fake welt pockets, make this vest a vest for all occasions. The number of regular buttonholes and buttons used has been reduced for simplicity and the fake welt pockets are placed centered over the princess seams on each side of the vest front. The bias-bound armholes complete the look.

The sample vest was made from the following materials:
   Fabric one: dobby weave fabric, olive/rust
   Decorative buttons: brown/brass (6)

Actual vest shown on page 101

. . . adding
patch pockets
with pocket flaps

Pauline Locke

. . . adding patch pockets with pocket flaps

. . . adding a mandarin collar & patch pockets

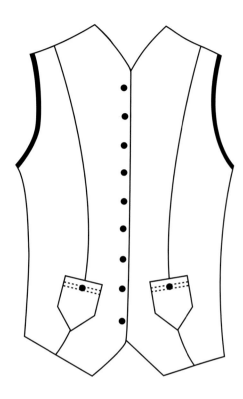

Artist's rendition of vest
shown on page 103

Ordinary patch pockets with points at the bottom complete this vest along with the frogs that have been added at the buttonholes. Several tiny buttonholes and buttons have been used along the vest front to add drama. In addition, tiny buttons are added on each pocket just below the pocket flap. The bias-bound armholes complete the look.

Artist's rendition of vest
shown on page 105

The mandarin collar and patch pockets that have been added to the basic vest redesign it into a unique waist-coat style vest. Bias binding around the armholes completes the look and the topstitching around the vest front and bottom edges and around the pockets adds dimension and interest. Fewer buttons have been used on this vest to maintain a comfortable styling.

. . . adding
a rounded
collar &
rounded
patch
pockets

. . . adding a rounded collar & rounded patch pockets

moments in time

enlarge all patterns 285%

Artist's rendition of vest shown on page 106

This waist-coat style vest with a rounded collar and rounded patch pockets takes the look back in time to the days of fitted, but comfortable and feminine, but modest. The princess seams add to the qualities of this vest and several tiny buttonholes and buttons also add detailing that cannot go unnoticed. The collar ends at the shoulders and the bias binding around the armholes is simple yet important to finish this fun-loving vest.

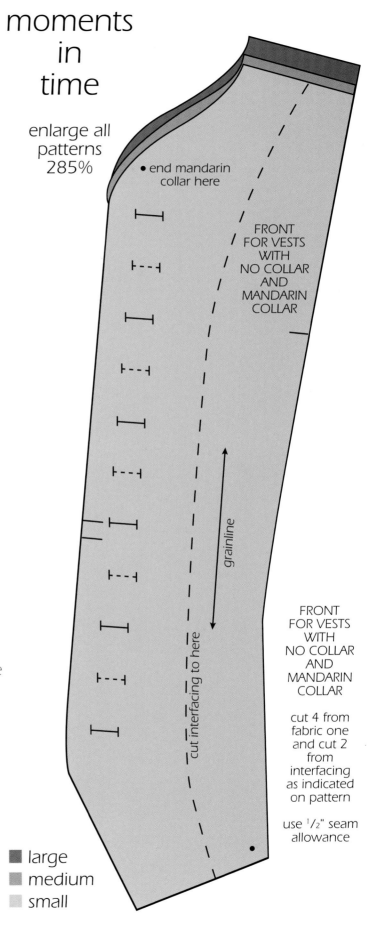

• end mandarin collar here

FRONT FOR VESTS WITH NO COLLAR AND MANDARIN COLLAR

grainline

cut interfacing to here

FRONT FOR VESTS WITH NO COLLAR AND MANDARIN COLLAR

cut 4 from fabric one and cut 2 from interfacing as indicated on pattern

use $1/2$" seam allowance

■ large
■ medium
■ small

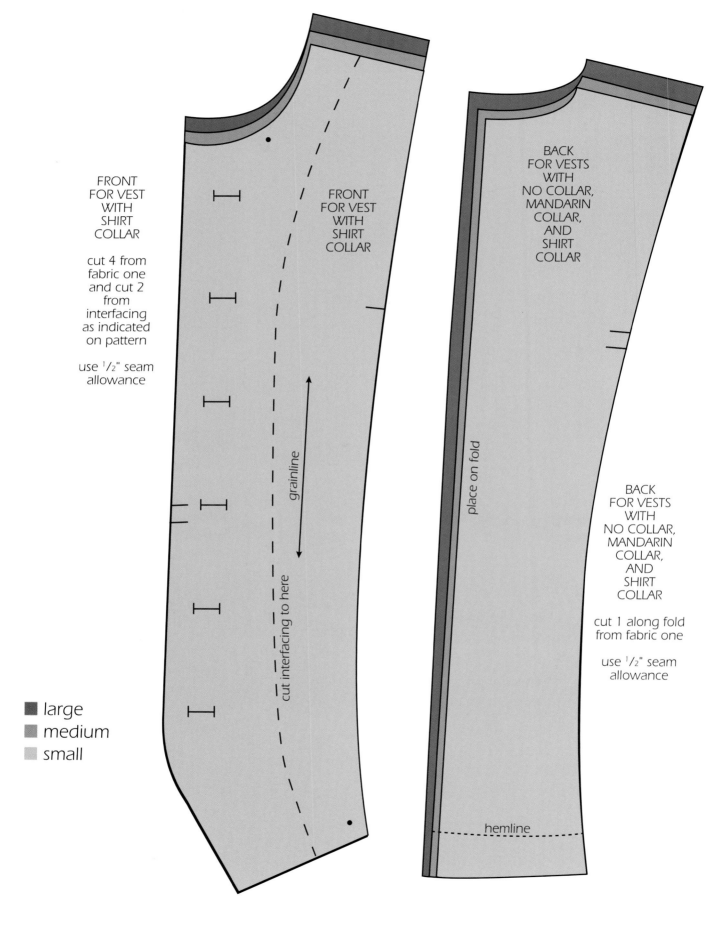

FRONT
FOR VEST
WITH
SHIRT
COLLAR

cut 4 from
fabric one
and cut 2
from
interfacing
as indicated
on pattern

use ¹/₂" seam
allowance

FRONT
FOR VEST
WITH
SHIRT
COLLAR

grainline

cut interfacing to here

■ large
■ medium
■ small

BACK
FOR VESTS
WITH
NO COLLAR,
MANDARIN
COLLAR,
AND
SHIRT
COLLAR

place on fold

BACK
FOR VESTS
WITH
NO COLLAR,
MANDARIN
COLLAR,
AND
SHIRT
COLLAR

cut 1 along fold
from fabric one

use ¹/₂" seam
allowance

hemline

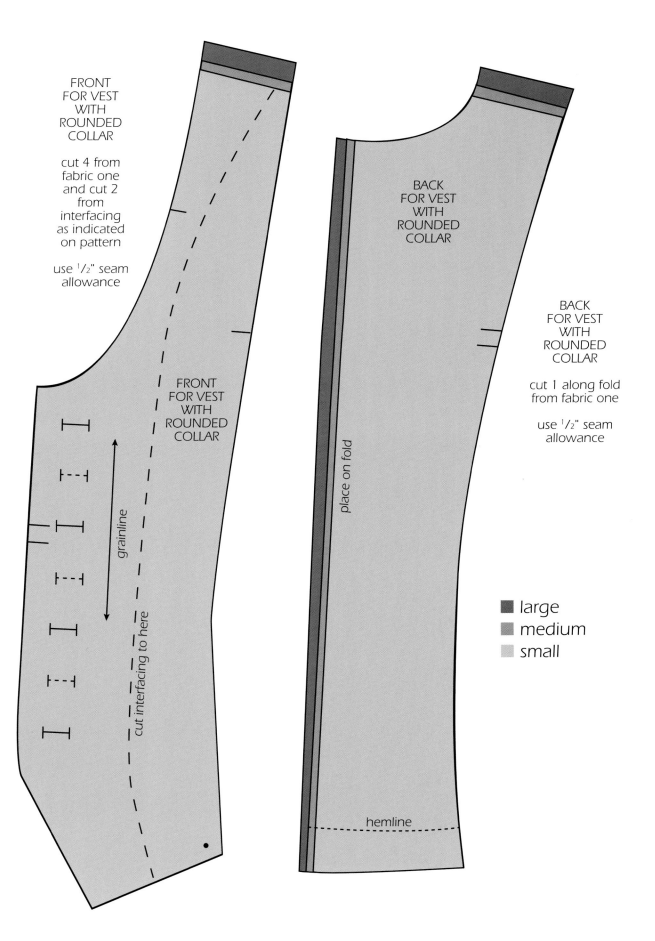

FRONT
FOR VEST
WITH
ROUNDED
COLLAR

cut 4 from
fabric one
and cut 2
from
interfacing
as indicated
on pattern

use ¹/₂" seam
allowance

FRONT
FOR VEST
WITH
ROUNDED
COLLAR

grainline

cut interfacing to here

BACK
FOR VEST
WITH
ROUNDED
COLLAR

BACK
FOR VEST
WITH
ROUNDED
COLLAR

cut 1 along fold
from fabric one

use ¹/₂" seam
allowance

place on fold

hemline

■ large
■ medium
■ small

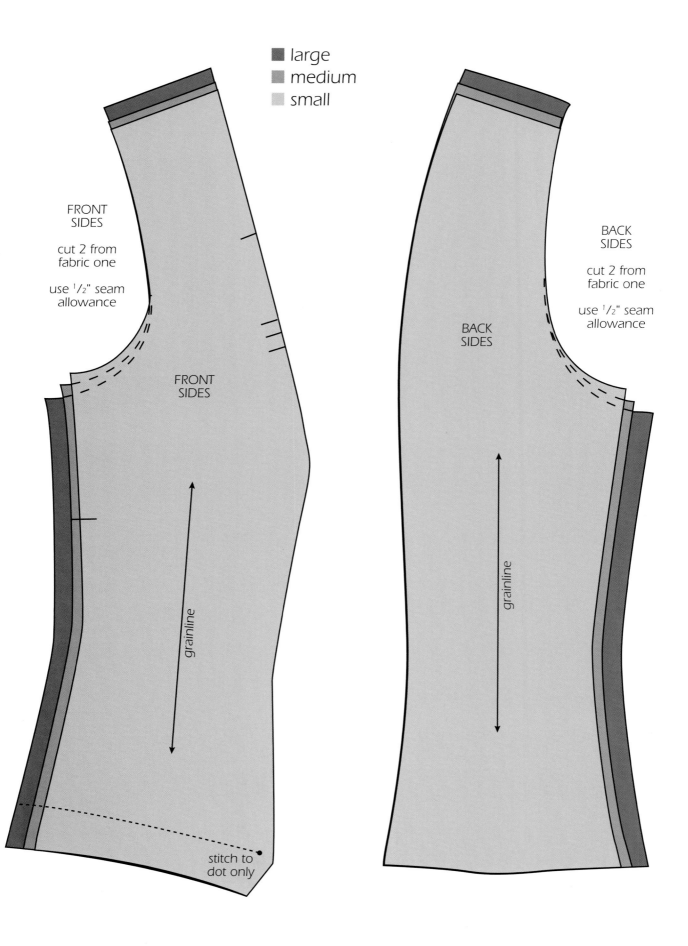

large
medium
small

FRONT
SIDES

cut 2 from
fabric one

use $1/2$" seam
allowance

FRONT
SIDES

grainline

stitch to
dot only

BACK
SIDES

BACK
SIDES

cut 2 from
fabric one

use $1/2$" seam
allowance

grainline

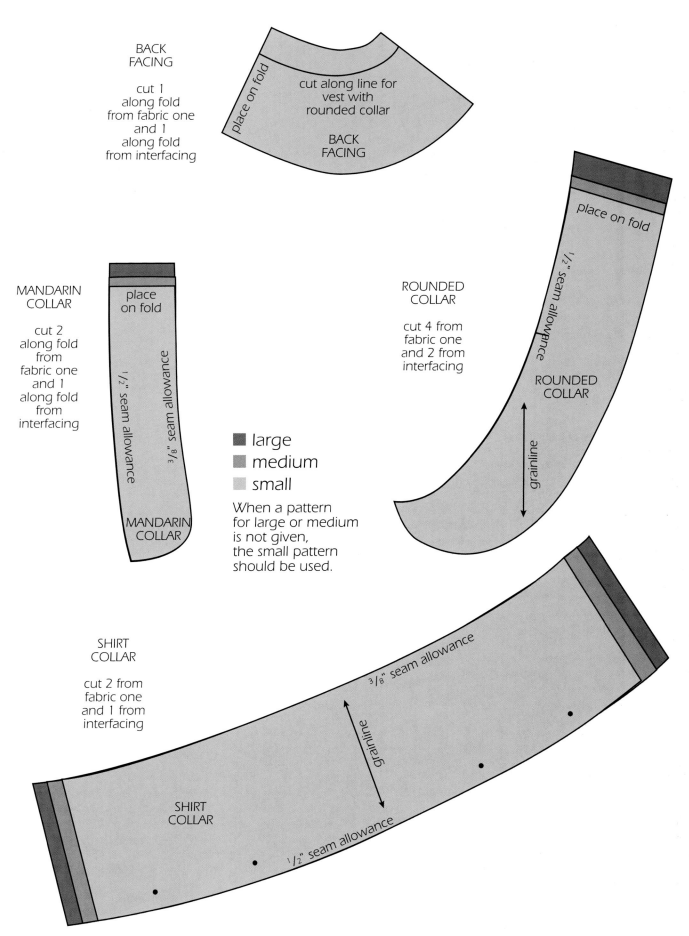

BACK
FACING

cut 1
along fold
from fabric one
and 1
along fold
from interfacing

place on fold

cut along line for
vest with
rounded collar

BACK
FACING

MANDARIN
COLLAR

cut 2
along fold
from
fabric one
and 1
along fold
from
interfacing

place
on fold

$1/2$" seam allowance

$3/8$" seam allowance

MANDARIN
COLLAR

large
medium
small

When a pattern
for large or medium
is not given,
the small pattern
should be used.

ROUNDED
COLLAR

cut 4 from
fabric one
and 2 from
interfacing

place on fold

$1/2$" seam allowance

ROUNDED
COLLAR

grainline

SHIRT
COLLAR

cut 2 from
fabric one
and 1 from
interfacing

$3/8$" seam allowance

grainline

SHIRT
COLLAR

$1/2$" seam allowance

dream scape . . .
the basic vest

dream scape

Deep in our hearts
we all long to be artists.
We want to capture the
dream scapes of fantasy
and share them
with the world.
In this long flowing vest,
you can express
the eccentricity
that is just
one thought away.

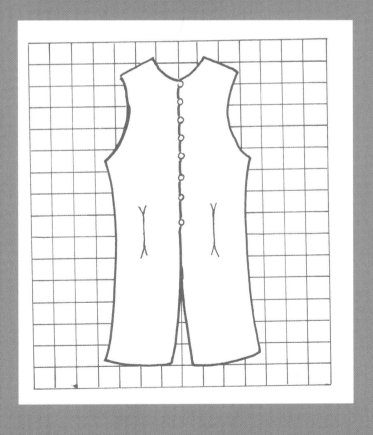

dream scape . . .
the basic vest

dream scape

materials needed

fabric one:
  44"-wide,
  $1^1/_2$ yards
  54"- to 60"-wide,
  1 yard
fusible interfacing:
  18"-wide,
  $^7/_8$ yard
buttons:
  decorative,
  $^1/_2$" (8)

IMPORTANT:

• Before beginning, it is recommended that you carefully read "learning the basics" on pages 5-21 and "collars & pockets" on pages 22-33.

• Yardages have been calculated for making the basic vest in a medium size. Adjust yardage amounts accordingly for collars, pockets, and variations in size or fabric usage.

1. cutting fabrics

fabric one:
  front, cut 2
  back, cut 2
  front facing,
    cut 2
  cut 1"-wide
    bias strips, 20"
fusible interfacing:
  front facing,
    cut 2

• Transfer all markings from pattern to vest pieces.

• Stitch vest in an assembly line manner for speedier results.

2. preparing vest pieces

Trim front facing interfacing pieces so there is a $^1/_8$" seam allowance on all edges.

Fuse interfacing to front facing pieces.

When adding lace to the fabric, overlay lace pieces onto the base cloth fabric. Pin and baste-stitch in place, then proceed with construction as with one cloth.

When adding a mandarin collar, trim collar interfacing pieces so there is a $^1/_8$" seam allowance on all edges. Fuse interfacing to the wrong sides of collar pieces.

Prepare collar at this time according to instructions on pages 23-28.

When adding pockets, fuse the interfacing to the wrong side of the pocket pieces.

Prepare pockets at this time according to instructions on pages 29-32.

3. stitching beginning vest elements

Follow instructions on pages 17-18 and pages 29-32 to add patch pockets to vest fronts.

Stitch back darts. Press darts toward center back.

Stitch front tucks and press toward the center.

Stitch back seam, right sides together, taking a $^1/_2$" seam allowance. For a clean finish, stitch back seam as a French seam. Press the French seam toward the right back.

Press the back hem up $^3/_4$" to the wrong side. Turn the raw edge under $^1/_4$" and stitch the hem in place and press.

4. making button loops & stitching front facing

When making fabric button loops, fold 1"-wide bias strip in half, matching long edges. Stitch $1/8$" in from folded edge, widening stitches to $1/4$" at the end of the strip. Insert a loop turner through loop opening, exiting turner at wider end. Latch the turner to fabric and turn fabric inside out through the tube, creating "spaghetti."

Baste-stitch "spaghetti" trim to the right front edge on button loop placement lines. Make loops $5/8$" deep.

Turn, press, and stitch the long, unnotched, edge of the front facing under $1/4$".

Stitch front facing to the neck, front, and hem edge of front, taking a $1/2$" seam allowance. At hem edge, take a $3/4$" seam allowance.

Trim seam along front edge and clip bulk from corners. Trim seam allowance on facings only at neck and hem edges. Turn right side out.

Press front edge seam allowances toward the facings.

Press the remaining front hem up $3/4$" to the wrong side. Turn raw edge under $1/4$" and stitch hem in place, stitching through the front facings as well. Press.

When adding a mandarin collar, proceed with step 5, prior to step 4.

When adding an exposed separating zipper, pin and stitch finished vest front edge directly next to the zipper teeth, aligning hem and neck edges. Finish neck according to step 6.

5. stitching vest front to back

Stitch front to back at shoulder seams, right sides together, taking a $1/2$" seam allowance. For a clean finish, stitch French seams. Press seams open. Press French seams toward back.

When adding a mandarin collar, stitch edge of top collar only to neck edge, matching notches, shoulder marks, and center back. Stitch, taking a $1/2$" seam allowance. Press seam toward collar. Proceed with step 4.

To finish collar neck edge, clip undercollar to seam at front facing. Turn remaining collar edge under $1/2$" and pin in place to encase neck edge. Stitch close to seam.

Stitch sides, right sides together, taking a $1/2$" seam allowance and ending at the dots. Press seam open.

6. finishing

Narrowly hem remaining side seams and press. Turn side seams under $1/8$" and stitch close to the folded edge for a clean finish.

Narrowly machine-stitch neck edge and armhole edges. Press thoroughly.

For the ribbon-embellished vest, hand-stitch picot-edge trim to front and back at neck edge.

Cut 7mm gray ribbon in half. Fray fibers from an end from one length of ribbon. Pull a center fiber to gather the ribbon. Position and pin gathered ribbon to left front neck edge in a random manner. Hand-stitch ribbon in place. Repeat with remaining ribbon length and right front neck edges. Press lightly.

Stitch buttons in place on left front.

the
basic vest . . .

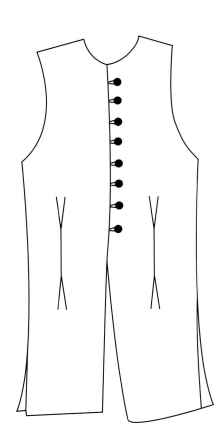

This long vest with buttons going half way down is a versatile garment for the woman on-the-go. It can be worn over any blouse or turtleneck or worn without anything underneath. A slit in the bottom of the side seams serves to prevent restriction of movement. The buttons are placed on the left front of the vest and loops are made.

The sample vest was made from the following materials:
Fabric one: cotton/polyester blend, Christmas print
Decorative buttons: metal poinsettias

Actual vest shown on pages 112 & 114

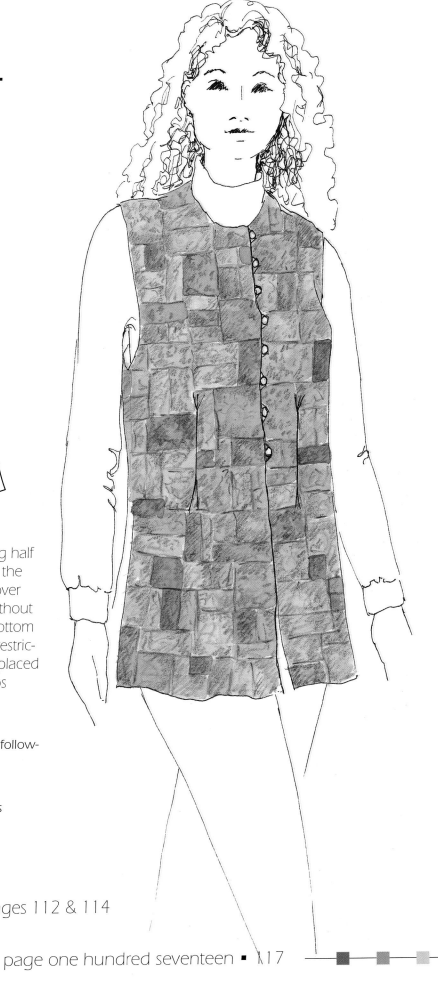

. . . changing
the neckline &
adding
ribbon trim

. . . changing the neckline & adding ribbon trim

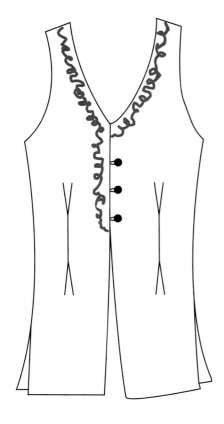

Changing the neckline on this vest from the basic vest changes this simple, everyday vest into a more elegant vest. The slight curve to the "V" and the ribbon trim added around the neckline and partially down the front of the vest give it a look of provocativeness, while still offering modesty. A slit in the bottom of the side seams serves to prevent restriction of movement. Fewer buttons have been added to this vest for a softer look. All edges have been hemmed for a nice finish.

The sample vest was made from the following materials:
Fabric one: base cloth, taupe
Fabric two: chantilly lace, lavender/gray
Trim: silk ribbon, gray; picot-edge trim, gray
Decorative buttons: mauve glass (3)

Actual vest shown on page 118

. . . adding
a mandarin
collar

. . . adding a mandarin collar

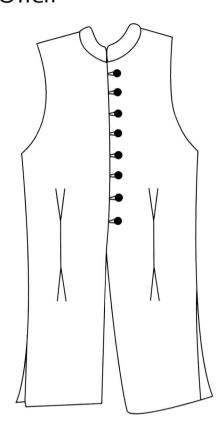

Artist's rendition of vest
shown on page 120

Adding a mandarin collar to the basic vest tends to dress-up this vest, however its versatility remains. A slit in the bottom of the side seams serves to prevent restriction of movement. The buttons are placed on the left front of the vest and loops are made. If desired, regular button-holes and buttons can be used. All edges have been hemmed for a nice finish.

. . . changing the neckline

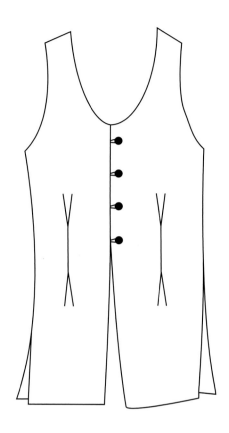

Artist's rendition of vest
shown on page 122

The scoop neck on this vest has been altered from the basic vest to reveal a little more of the chest area. A slit in the bottom of the side seams serves to prevent restriction of movement. The buttons are placed on the left front of the vest and loops are made, but fewer buttons have been used to make the vest a little more casual. If desired, regular buttonholes and buttons can be used. All edges have been hemmed for a nice finish.

. . . changing
the neckline